C000138673

Humanitarian Report 1997

UNITED NATIONS
ew York and Geneva, 1997

NOTE

Symbols of United Nations documents are composed of capital letters combined with figures. Mention of such a symbol indicates a reference to a United Nations document.

The designations employed and the presentation of the material in this publication do not imply the expression of any opinion whatsoever on the part of the Secretariat of the United Nations concerning the legal status of any country, territory, city or area, or of its authorities, or concerning the delimitation of its frontiers or boundaries.

DHA/97/72

UNITED NATIONS PUBLICATION
Sales No. GV.E.97.0.11
ISBN 92-1-100745-3

Foreword

by the Secretary-General

Humanitarian tragedies occur every day of the year in all corners of the world. No matter what their cause—a flood or internal conflict—they claim lives and leave in their wake material devastation and untold suffering. Many of the victims become displaced within their countries or are obliged to seek asylum abroad.

When natural disasters strike, their impact in developing countries is particularly severe. Mortality figures in these countries account for the vast majority of the total. There can be no doubt that poverty, population pressures and environmental degradation exacerbate the degree of destruction, and contribute significantly to large-scale economic losses and disruption of social institutions.

We have also witnessed in the past decade an upsurge in the number and intensity of internal conflicts, which are marked by massive displacements of people, extensive violence and loss of life, and widespread damage to the affected societies and economies. These conflicts do not occur in a vacuum. To end them, we must look to the causes and address them in a forthright manner. We have the responsibility for helping all parties to a conflict reach a peaceful settlement that they can support over the long term.

But while these conflicts rage, we must take urgent measures to alleviate the pain of the victims, both by meeting their most urgent requirements for food, clean water, medicines, shelter and other humanitarian relief, and by assisting them in rebuilding the destroyed structures of civil society.

Experience has shown that once a humanitarian emergency has occurred, the international community moves swiftly to address the suffering of the victims. In the five years since the General Assembly called for a more coordinated system of humanitarian response, much progress has been made in mobilizing the collective efforts of the international community to deliver assistance in a coherent and timely manner. Under the leadership of the Emergency Relief Coordinator, DHA and organizations of the United Nations system, including the United Nations Children's Fund, the United Nations Development Programme, the World Food Programme, the United Nations High Commissioner for Refugees, the World Health Organization and the Food and Agriculture Organization of the United Nations, together with their humanitarian partners—donors, the International Red Cross and Red Crescent Movement, the International Organization for Migration, non-governmental organizations and other concerned parties—have raised billions of dollars to deliver relief assistance to the needy. Most of those receiving such aid are children, women and the elderly.

Assistance is provided in spite of the major constraints that face humanitarian workers in the field. These range from difficulty in reaching populations in need to lack of security and, often, to a total disregard for the fundamental principles of international humanitarian law and human rights. I remain gravely concerned by the recent increase in attacks on, and the use of force against, relief personnel, which in some cases have been carried out by groups with the deliberate goal of hampering humanitarian access.

Such problems point to the inextricable connection between the manifestation of the problem—a man-made or natural disaster and the humanitarian imperative to save the lives of innocent victims—and the underlying causes, which are political, military, economic, social and environmental. However important humanitarian assistance may be in saving lives, it can only be a palliative. The political will and requisite resources must be directed towards finding a lasting cure.

We must develop a holistic vision that integrates all these elements and seeks to break the cycle of violence and human suffering. We must continue to strengthen our early-warning and early-response mechanisms to prevent identifiable threats from becoming terrible realities in disaster-prone countries and those on the brink of civil conflict. We must also ensure preventive action through development and diplomatic efforts.

I am pleased to introduce the *Humanitarian Report 1997*, which highlights the magnitude of the challenge and demonstrates the accomplishments of the humanitarian community. I also wish to take this opportunity to pay a special tribute to the staff of the United Nations, as well as of other humanitarian organizations, including the International Committee of the Red Cross, the International Federation of Red Cross and Red Crescent Societies and international and local non-governmental organizations. These women and men should be commended for their tireless and courageous efforts, under extremely difficult conditions, to alleviate the burden of suffering in the world■

Kofi ANNAN
Secretary-General of the United Nations

Contents

Page

Introduction **1**

PART ONE
Evolution of humanitarian coordination 1992-1997

Chapter

1. Humanitarian coordination in complex emergencies and natural disasters **9**
Coordination before and after 1992 9
DHA: mission and priorities 10
Coordination at the headquarters level 12
Coordination in the field 14
Boxes: The Disaster Management Training Programme 13
Coordination structure in Sierra Leone 16

2. Resource mobilization **19**
Fund-raising for complex emergencies 19
Fund-raising for natural and technological disasters 24

3. Information in humanitarian response **30**
Early warning system 31
Regional/country information networks 31
A global information platform 32

PART TWO
Major developments in emergency relief coordination, 1996-early 1997: complex emergencies and natural disasters

4. The Great Lakes Region of Central Africa **37**
Box: Lessons from the Rwanda experience 43

5. Afghanistan **44**
Box: Gender issues in Afghanistan 48

6. The Sudan **49**
Boxes: Assessing the humanitarian impact of sanctions on the Sudan ... 50
Plan of Action Implementing Operation Lifeline Sudan Review ... 54

7. Iraq: the humanitarian programme and the implementation of Security Council resolution 986 (1995) ... **55**

8. Demobilization in Angola and Liberia **60**

9. Major natural, technological and environmental disasters **67**
Disaster response mechanisms 67
DHA response to major disasters in 1996: Democratic People's Republic of Korea; China; Central America; Yemen; and the Philippines 68

Contents *(continued)*

PART THREE
Continuing challenges for humanitarian coordination

Chapter	*Page*
10. The reduction of natural, technological and environmental disasters	**73**
Costs and causes	73
Reducing natural disasters	77
Reducing technological disasters	81
Boxes: Regional priorities in reducing natural, technological and environmental disasters	75
Protecting cities at risk	81
The Chernobyl disaster	82
11. The global scourge of anti-personnel landmines	**86**
Priorities for United Nations mine-clearance	87
DHA role in humanitarian demining	88
Towards a global ban on anti-personnel landmines	93
Boxes: A summary of mine action activities in Bosnia and Herzegovina	89
Major conferences towards a global ban on landmines	96
12. Internally displaced people	**98**
The causes and categories of internal displacement	98
The special problems of IDPs	98
Institutional developments	99
13. The link between relief and development	**103**
Aligning development objectives with humanitarian principles	103
The evolving consensus	104
Box: South Caucasus: resource constraints on relief and development	106

ANNEXES

Annex	
I. DHA representatives in the field	107
II. Recent DHA publications and training materials	108

List of maps

Map	
I. DHA emergency response: 1996-31 March 1997	4-5
II. Population movements in the Great Lakes Region	38
III. Population movements in Afghanistan	45
IV. United Nations/OLS emergency programmes in the Sudan	53
V. Humanitarian Programme in Iraq	58
VI. Quartering sites in Angola	62
VII. Disarmament and demobilization sites in Liberia	64
VIII. Caesium deposits in Europe after the Chernobyl accident	84
IX. Landmine risk in Bosnia and Herzegovina: 1996	91
X. Landmine incidents in Sarajevo: 1992-1996	92
XI. United Nations landmine programmes: 1994 to 31 March 1997	94-95
XII. Significant populations of displaced persons: 1996	100-101

Introduction

I am pleased to introduce *Humanitarian Report 1997*, produced by the United Nations Department of Humanitarian Affairs (DHA) to reflect the main developments and trends in the area of emergency and disaster assistance in the five years since the establishment of the Department.

The Report describes how the basic mechanisms of humanitarian coordination have evolved since the United Nations Secretary-General, in response to General Assembly resolution 46/182, appointed an Emergency Relief Coordinator and established the Department of Humanitarian Affairs in March 1992. The Report also details the international response in 1996 and the first quarter of 1997, to major humanitarian emergencies—notably those in the Great Lakes Region of Central Africa, Afghanistan, the Sudan, Iraq, Angola, and Liberia—as well as to major natural disasters.[1] In the final section, the Report analyses several of the continuing challenges which confront the international humanitarian community: containing and reducing the human and material damage and costs of natural, technological and environmental disasters; confronting the humanitarian consequences of anti-personnel landmines; meeting the special needs of internally-displaced persons; and moving beyond humanitarian relief to support the longer-term goals of sustainable political, economic and social development.

These past five years have demonstrated the timeliness of the General Assembly's call for increased coordination and closer cooperation among the international humanitarian organizations. The primary role of the Emergency Relief Coordinator, together with the Inter-Agency Standing Committee, has been to develop a coherent approach to the delivery of humanitarian assistance which reflects a shared analysis of a

---

[1] Factual material in this report concentrates on the period 1 January 1996 to the end of March/mid-April 1997.

FIGURE 1. *Under-Secretary-General Yasushi Akashi inspects bags of wheat flour in a World Food Programme warehouse in Mosul, Iraq (5 May 1997).*

given crisis. Such a coordinated approach must encourage interactions among the United Nations' humanitarian agencies, Member States, other intergovernmental organizations, the International Red Cross and Red Crescent Movement, and international and local non-governmental organizations, both in the field and at headquarters. It must combine the humanitarian community's assessments of the needs in a given crisis, mobilize the necessary resources, and pool information so as to ensure early, timely and effective response. As the Emergency Relief Coordinator, I share the perspectives of the humanitarian community with the Secretary-General, the intergovernmental organs of the United Nations, and governments and citizens around the world; and communicate to the humanitarian community the actions and policies of the Secretary-General and the intergovernmental organs that pertain to emergency relief.

Over the past five years, the international community has supported large-scale humanitarian operations in countries devastated by political turmoil, internal conflicts and major

disasters. Aid workers from many agencies and organizations have followed the imperative to help victims according to the established principles of impartial humanitarian action. Millions of the most vulnerable and needy have been given food, shelter and medical care. Tens of thousands of lost children have been reunited with their families. Millions of refugees have been returned to their original homes or resettled in new communities. Many war-torn economies and societies are being repaired and confidence is being built among long-hostile neighbours.

Disasters and emergencies have complex origins and rarely have a purely humanitarian solution. Emergency assistance cannot be a substitute for political action to address the root causes of the crisis. If a society does not provide its people with basic security in their home communities, does not secure fundamental human rights, does not protect ethnic minorities, does not ensure at least some prospect of sustainable political, economic and social development, and does not provide a disaster-resistant environment, then there is the potential for a disaster or emergency with serious humanitarian consequences.

How to tailor humanitarian action to the conditions prevailing in today's conflict zones, so that it strengthens and not weakens the capacities of the local communities and is supportive of longer-term development, is a continuing challenge. When people are forcibly uprooted and expelled from their homes, when the aim of warfare is to inflict maximum pain, when groups of people are attacked solely because of their ethnic, religious or national character, where civilians are directly targeted and where the work of relief agencies is deliberately obstructed, protection requirements are different from what is needed in more traditional humanitarian assistance operations. There is a growing recognition that security, first and foremost, concerns the well-being of people and is not of lesser value than the security of States. Increasingly, the concept of sovereignty is being linked to the ability of States to respect and safeguard the security of their citizens.

Just as humanitarian action must be tailored to the political and security situation in zones of conflict, effective humanitarian action must also serve the objective of longer-term, sustainable development. Effective emergency response requires that the seeds of development be planted at the same time that relief needs are addressed, since it is in the volatile conditions of an emergency or the aftermath of a major disaster that community-building and accountability can be initiated or renewed. These building blocks of recovery must go hand in hand with simultaneous attention to a wide range of economic, social and political issues: restoring social services, infrastructure and food production systems; economic revival and job creation; demobilization and reintegration of combatants; the development of a functioning legal system; and the encouragement of constitutional development and human rights. These elements of recovery cannot await what some might term ''appropriate'' conditions for long-term development; they constitute the bridge between relief and development. Concern about these issues must infuse the humanitarian response from the outset of the crisis and well on into the recovery period.

The challenge for us in the face of this situation is to strengthen humanitarian coordination and enhance the international community's ability and will to forge comprehensive solutions to humanitarian problems. Such solutions would incorporate the political, security, social and economic elements without which humanitarian aid alone can accomplish little of lasting value. I would wish to pay a tribute to my predecessors as Emergency Relief Coordinator, Jan Eliasson, now State Secretary, Ministry of Foreign Affairs of Sweden, and Peter Hansen, now Commissioner-General of the United Nations Relief and Works Agency for Palestine Refugees in the Near East, for the hard work they undertook to identify such comprehensive solutions.

In carrying out our tasks, we have been able to count upon the steadfast work of thousands of dedicated humanitarian workers from many nations. I sincerely thank them and convey to them our deepest appreciation for their efforts, often at great danger to themselves, to meet the needs of victims throughout the world ■

Yasushi AKASHI
Under-Secretary-General for Humanitarian Affairs

International humanitarian organizations

I. The United Nations

The United Nations funds/programmes/agencies with primary roles in emergencies and disasters are:

The United Nations Children's Fund (UNICEF)

UNICEF provides assistance, particularly health, safe water and sanitation, nutrition and education, to children and women in developing countries and to victims of emergencies and disasters. UNICEF has country programme agreements with 145 countries. Its budget for 1996 was US$ 944 million, of which US$ 145 million was for humanitarian assistance.

The United Nations Development Programme (UNDP)

UNDP is the United Nations' largest provider of grants for development and the central coordinating body for United Nations technical cooperation. It works with 174 countries and territories through offices in 134 countries. Contributions and pledges to UNDP for 1996 amounted to approximately US$ 2 billion, of which US$ 23.5 million was for emergency humanitarian assistance. UNDP also manages the United Nations resident coordinator function. Resident coordinators often serve as United Nations humanitarian coordinators in countries in crisis.

The United Nations High Commissioner for Refugees (UNHCR)

UNHCR is mandated to protect, repatriate and resettle refugees and also provides humanitarian assistance. In some cases it also coordinates assistance programmes for internally displaced persons. As of February 1997, UNHCR had 239 offices in 119 countries. Its 1996 budget was US$ 1.145 billion.

The World Food Programme (WFP)

WFP provides food to sustain victims of emergencies and disasters, to improve the nutrition of the most vulnerable people, and to promote the self-reliance of poor people and communities. In 1996 it had operational activities in 84 countries and its expenditures amounted to US$ 1.2 billion, of which approximately US$ 875 million was for relief activities.

Other United Nations agencies which play important roles in emergencies and disasters are:

The Food and Agriculture Organization of the United Nations (FAO)

The High Commissioner for Human Rights/Centre for Human Rights (HCHR/CHR)

The United Nations Centre for Human Settlements (UNCHS or Habitat)

The United Nations Educational, Scientific and Cultural Organization (UNESCO)

The United Nations Office for Project Services (UNOPS)

The United Nations Relief and Works Agency for Palestine Refugees in the Near East (UNRWA)

The World Health Organization (WHO)

II. Other international organizations

The International Organization for Migration (IOM)

IOM arranges resettlement and repatriation for refugees, internally displaced persons and migrants. It is present in approximately 175 countries. In 1996 its budget was US$ 251 million, of which US$ 152 million was for humanitarian migration assistance.

(Continued on page 6.)

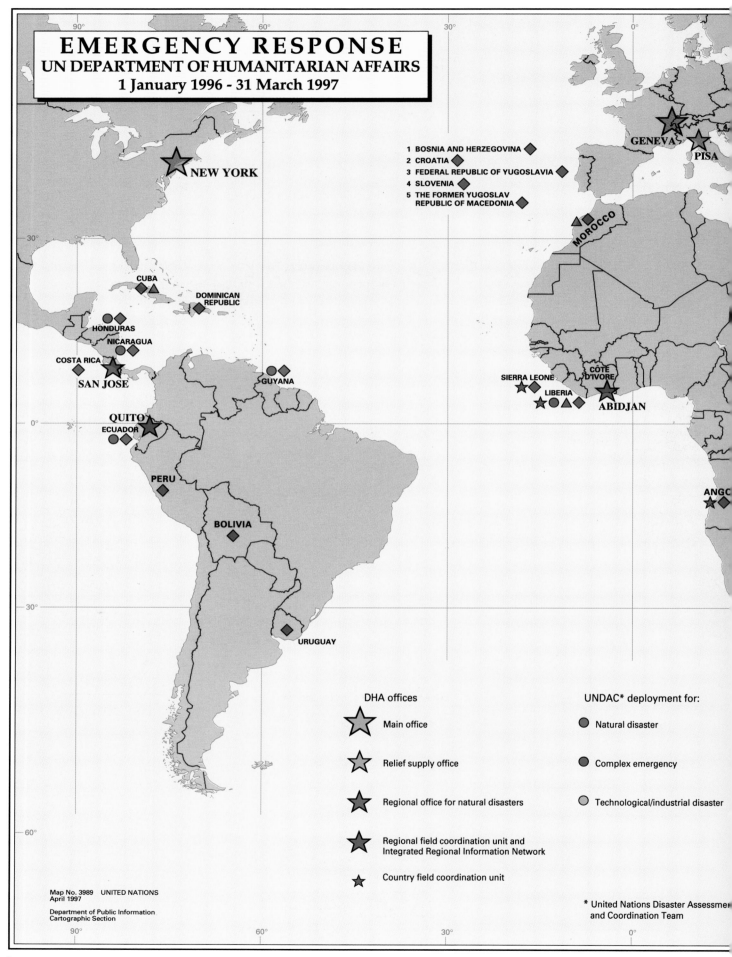

EMERGENCY RESPONSE
UN DEPARTMENT OF HUMANITARIAN AFFAIRS
1 January 1996 - 31 March 1997

NEW YORK

1 BOSNIA AND HERZEGOVINA ◆
2 CROATIA ◆
3 FEDERAL REPUBLIC OF YUGOSLAVIA ◆
4 SLOVENIA ◆
5 THE FORMER YUGOSLAV
REPUBLIC OF MACEDONIA ◆

GENEVA

PISA

MOROCCO

CUBA

DOMINICAN
REPUBLIC

HONDURAS

NICARAGUA

COSTA RICA

SAN JOSE

GUYANA

SIERRA LEONE

CÔTE
D'IVOIRE

LIBERIA

ABIDJAN

QUITO

ECUADOR

PERU

BOLIVIA

ANGO

URUGUAY

DHA offices

★ Main office

★ Relief supply office

★ Regional office for natural disasters

★ Regional field coordination unit and
Integrated Regional Information Network

★ Country field coordination unit

UNDAC* deployment for:

● Natural disaster

● Complex emergency

○ Technological/industrial disaster

* United Nations Disaster Assessment
and Coordination Team

Map No. 3989   UNITED NATIONS
April 1997

Department of Public Information
Cartographic Section

4

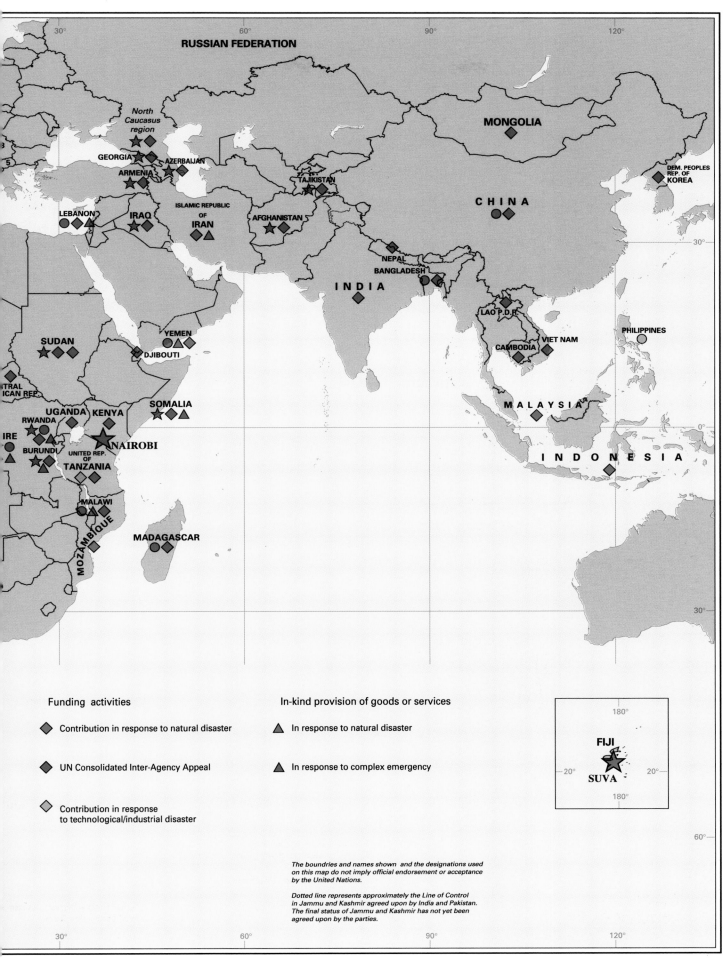

RUSSIAN FEDERATION

North Caucasus region

GEORGIA
ARMENIA
AZERBAIJAN
TAJIKISTAN
MONGOLIA
DEM. PEOPLES REP. OF KOREA

LEBANON
IRAQ
ISLAMIC REPUBLIC OF IRAN
AFGHANISTAN
C H I N A

NEPAL
BANGLADESH
I N D I A

SUDAN
YEMEN
DJIBOUTI
LAO P.D.R.
VIET NAM
CAMBODIA
PHILIPPINES

TRAL ICAN REP.
UGANDA KENYA
RWANDA
IRE
BURUNDI
NAIROBI
UNITED REP. OF TANZANIA
SOMALIA
M A L A Y S I A

I N D O N E S I A

MALAWI
MOZAMBIQUE
MADAGASCAR

Funding activities

◆ Contribution in response to natural disaster

◆ UN Consolidated Inter-Agency Appeal

◇ Contribution in response to technological/industrial disaster

In-kind provision of goods or services

▲ In response to natural disaster

▲ In response to complex emergency

FIJI
SUVA

The boundaries and names shown and the designations used on this map do not imply official endorsement or acceptance by the United Nations.

Dotted line represents approximately the Line of Control in Jammu and Kashmir agreed upon by India and Pakistan. The final status of Jammu and Kashmir has not yet been agreed upon by the parties.

(Continued from page 3.)

The European Community Humanitarian Office (ECHO)

ECHO, the Humanitarian Office of the European Union (EU), manages and coordinates all EU relief efforts. In 1996 it provided ECU 903 million, or US$ 1.2 billion, in humanitarian assistance.

III. The International Red Cross and Red Crescent Movement

The International Red Cross and Red Crescent Movement comprises the International Committee of the Red Cross (ICRC), the International Federation of Red Cross and Red Crescent Societies (IFRC), and currently 179 national Red Cross and Red Crescent societies.

Founded in 1863, the ICRC is the oldest international humanitarian organization and the largest outside the United Nations system. In 1996, it maintained a presence in 54 countries and conducted operations in 80 countries. ICRC's expenditure in 1996 was 760 million Swiss francs (Sw F), approximately US$ 542 million.

Founded in 1919, the IFRC is the federation of 179 national Red Cross and Red Crescent societies. In 1996 IFRC raised SF 229 million, approximately US$ 164 million, for relief operations and programmes throughout the world.

IV. Non-governmental organizations (NGOs)

InterAction. InterAction is a coalition of over 150 US-based private non-profit agencies involved in development and relief assistance worldwide.

International Council of Voluntary Agencies (ICVA). ICVA is a consortium of almost 100 private relief and development organizations based in Africa, Asia and the Pacific, Europe, Latin America and North America.

Steering Committee for Humanitarian Response. The Steering Committee for Humanitarian response is an alliance of Care International, Caritas Internationalis, the International Federation of the Red Cross/Red Crescent Societies, the International Save the Children Alliance, Lutheran World Federation, Oxfam International, and the World Council of Churches. Médecins sans frontières recently became an observer.

Part One

Evolution of humanitarian coordination, 1992-1997

Chapter 1

Humanitarian coordination in complex emergencies and natural disasters

It is now universally acknowledged that effective coordination of humanitarian assistance is crucial for saving lives, helping victims and encouraging local coping mechanisms. Humanitarian emergency situations are characterized by widespread and urgent needs, competing priorities, destroyed or damaged infrastructure, a rapid influx of relief workers and humanitarian aid, and great pressure on national authorities and civic institutions. An emergency situation thus risks slipping into chaos.

Absence of or weak coordination in humanitarian crises could result in gaps in services to affected populations, duplication of efforts, inefficient use of resources, political and other impediments, and slow reactions to changing conditions. By contrast, effective coordination allows the range of entities involved in humanitarian efforts to harmonize their responses. When coordination works, humanitarian aid efforts become greater than the sum of their parts. It was this recognition that led to the establishment in 1992 of the United Nations Department of Humanitarian Affairs (DHA) to coordinate the provision of humanitarian assistance in emergencies and disasters.

Coordination before and after 1992

Before 1992, a number of efforts were made to coordinate United Nations humanitarian relief. For emergencies that clearly fell within the mandate and competence of a single agency—e.g. WFP for food shortages or UNHCR for refugee crises—the agency in question was expected to lead the United Nations response. For natural disasters, especially sudden-onset disasters such as earthquakes or tsunamis, the Office of the United Nations Disaster Relief Coordinator (UNDRO) helped disseminate information on relief needs and donor response, while in the affected country, United Nations relief efforts were normally coordinated by the United Nations Resident Coordinator.

Although not perfect, these mechanisms addressed many single-sector emergencies and natural disasters. The major shortcoming of these arrangements was in dealing with the complex humanitarian emergencies that were to become a feature of the post-cold-war era. A complex emergency is defined as:

"A humanitarian crisis in a country, region or society where there is a total or considerable breakdown of authority resulting from internal or external conflict and which requires an international response that goes beyond the mandate or capacity of any single agency and/or the ongoing UN country programme."[1]

Prior to 1992, the United Nations approach to coordinating humanitarian response to large complex emergencies was through ad hoc mechanisms, such as:

- the United Nations Border Relief Operation (UNBRO) for the Thai-Cambodia border in the 1980s;
- the Office of Emergency Operations for Africa for the drought of the mid-1980s; and
- Operation Lifeline Sudan, starting in 1989.

While many of these mechanisms proved valuable and useful, the effort required to create and operate them limited their application to only the largest, high-profile emergencies. The majority of complex emergencies—the lower-profile, or smaller-scale emergencies that fail to attract high-level policy or international media attention—did not engender comparable coordination efforts. The ad hoc approach had other negative consequences as well, such as:

- the need to "reinvent the wheel" for many aspects of each new emergency;
- no agreed, clear division of responsibilities and roles among the various players;
- disjointed resource mobilization efforts, resulting from appeals coming from individual agencies and organizations; and
- in most instances, the lack of an overall strategic vision for relief efforts, particularly at the outset of the crisis.

The year 1991 was a watershed in the debate over humanitarian coordination, for several reasons. The Kurdish crisis in northern Iraq and on the Iraq-Turkey border pointed to the urgent need for more effective coordination mechanisms. With the ending of the cold war, there was also a sense that the international community in general, and the United Nations in particular, could play a more important role in providing humanitarian assistance in complex emergencies. There was, as well, a growing recognition that such emergencies—most often rooted in internal armed conflicts—were not temporary, transient events, but rather, likely to be persistent features on the international landscape. In the aftermath of the cold war, complex emergencies appeared, if anything, to be increasing in number and scope.

In December 1991, the United Nations General Assembly adopted resolution 46/182. This resolution set out guiding principles for the coordination and provision of humanitarian assistance, putting particular emphasis on prevention and preparedness. It established the Inter-Agency

---

[1] "Working Paper on the Definition of Complex Emergency", Inter-Agency Standing Committee, December 1994.

Standing Committee (IASC) consisting of the heads of major United Nations agencies and other humanitarian organizations; set forth mechanisms for more rapid and effective humanitarian response; and called on the Secretary-General to designate an Emergency Relief Coordinator (ERC).

The resolution also resulted in the establishment of the Department of Humanitarian Affairs (DHA) to support the work of the Emergency Relief Coordinator appointed by the Secretary-General in April 1992. The newly created DHA, both located in New York and Geneva, subsumed certain United Nations structures dealing with emergency programmes, including those in Afghanistan, Iraq and the Sudan, as well as UNDRO. These arrangements were endorsed by the General Assembly in its resolution 47/168.

The DHA dual presence reflected the reality that humanitarian action, particularly in complex emergencies, is closely linked to political and military issues—and hence, to the Security Council, General Assembly and the Office of the Secretary-General in New York. At the same time, Geneva is a key humanitarian centre, where a number of major humanitarian agencies, such as UNHCR, WHO and ICRC have their headquarters. While the driving force behind the creation of DHA was the need for better coordination in complex emergencies, the need to strengthen aspects of the response to natural and other types of disasters was also acknowledged. Thus DHA was also given a mandate for coordinating the United Nations response to natural disasters, improving preparedness for, and mitigating the consequences of, natural and other disasters. (See figure 2 opposite.) Finally, DHA was mandated to work through, and build upon, the United Nations resident coordinator system in countries with emergency needs.

DHA: mission and priorities

The DHA mission, led by the ERC, is to mobilize and coordinate the efforts of the international community, in particular those of the United Nations system, so as to alleviate the human suffering and material destruction in disasters and emergencies through effective and timely assistance. It also seeks to reduce vulnerability, promote solutions to root causes, and build links between humanitarian relief and development. DHA's highest priorities are to:

* *Establish humanitarian policy and principles*

Work closely with other humanitarian partners to refine international humanitarian principles and norms, and to promote their adoption and application within each emergency or disaster. In pursuit of these objectives, play a leading role in shaping the international response to emergencies, and work with humanitarian, military and political actors to define further the appropriate roles and responsibilities of each sector.

* *Advocate humanitarian principles and concerns*

Aim its advocacy efforts at increasing respect for humanitarian principles, both generally, as well as in specific crises, through the promotion of such principles and the condemnation of violations. Ensure also that the humanitarian dimension is fully reflected in overall United Nations approaches to crisis situations, whether in the prevention, preparedness or response stage. Finally, promote understanding and support for humanitarian work in the international public arena.

* *Coordinate humanitarian actions*

In collaboration with other relevant actors, help formulate comprehensive strategies for specific emergencies which prioritize humanitarian requirements and allocate responsibilities among humanitarian partners. Develop guidelines and training programmes to facilitate inter-agency coordination and assessments. On a more technical level, seek to streamline rules and regulations, and to put into place procedures to allow for rapid and effective support for in-country coordination.

* *Strengthen capacity at local, national and international levels*

Strengthen national capacities to reduce vulnerability to disasters through continuing technical assistance to disaster-prone countries. In addition, working with humanitarian partners, conduct evaluation studies as well as implement the resulting recommendations, in order to improve local, national and international capacity in disaster prevention, preparedness, mitigation and response.

* *Mobilize resources*

Where appropriate, organize and lead joint efforts to mobilize resources to meet priority relief needs of the affected population, as well as for prevention, preparedness, mitigation and early recovery activities. For complex emergencies, this is done through the Consolidated Appeals Process (CAP).

* *Collect, analyse and disseminate information*

Ensure information on humanitarian needs and response is available to the international community on which to base sound policy, advocacy and decision-making. This is done through support of emergency information systems aimed at early warning, preventive action and timely response. Strengthen arrangements for the collection and dissemination of information relevant to field operations.

Substantial experience in humanitarian coordination since 1992 has helped clarify the nature of humanitarian coordination, and the best ways to promote it. Among these approaches are:

Facilitating cooperation. Coordination of humanitarian assistance is not based on some "chain of command" which mandates DHA to direct the actions of the United Nations humanitarian agencies, much less those of the wider humanitarian community. In practice, coordination requires cooperation among humanitarian partners. It should lead to concrete benefits: agreements among members of the IASC on the roles, policies, procedures and institutional mechanisms which constitute a working framework for coordination; the provision of useful services; and a genuine climate of cooperation among humanitarian partners. While involving more humanitarian partners can sometimes make decision-making more complicated, coordination efforts must be as inclusive as possible: reaching out beyond the traditional circle of United Nations agencies, other international organizations, and Governments, to the

DEPARTMENT OF HUMANITARIAN AFFAIRS

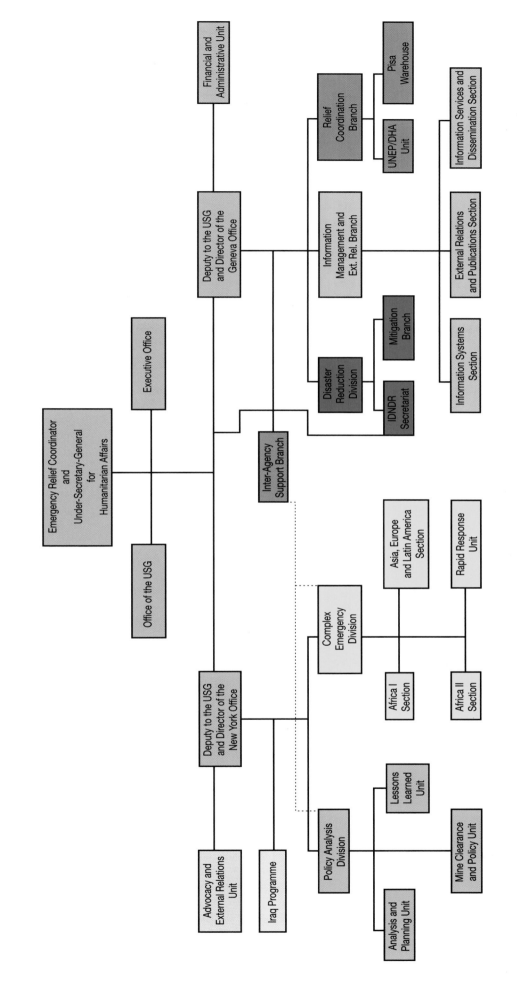

FIGURE 2. *Organigram showing the present structure of the United Nations Department of Humanitarian Affairs.*

wider humanitarian community, including the media and the affected populations themselves. It also entails dialogue and cooperation with other entities which have closely related concerns, such as human rights groups, and multilateral or national military forces.

Strengthening support for field coordination. The ultimate objective of most work done at DHA headquarters, as well as at the headquarters of the United Nations humanitarian agencies, is to support humanitarian efforts in the affected country. For DHA, a primary focus is to support the office of the United Nations Resident/Humanitarian Coordinator and the United Nations Disaster Management Team. DHA provides these field-based units with experienced staff, telecommunications and logistical support, start-up funds, and an effective flow of information. DHA also supports the Resident/Humanitarian Coordinator by articulating his/her concerns to United Nations bodies, interested Governments, and the public at large.

Promoting systemic improvements. DHA is committed to identifying and promoting improvements that can have an impact across the wider humanitarian assistance system. This requires learning the lessons of current and previous relief efforts, and identifying new opportunities for systemic change. Strengthening early warning capacities, utilizing new technologies for information-sharing, promoting demining activities and coordinating inter-agency disaster management training are examples of such systemic improvements (see box opposite).

Coordination at the headquarters level

United Nations humanitarian coordination involves interactions among a large number and range of actors. These include:

- United Nations humanitarian agencies, such as UNHCR, UNICEF, WFP, UNDP and others;
- Other international humanitarian organizations such as IOM and ICRC;
- International humanitarian NGOs;

- Relevant United Nations entities such as the Office of the Secretary-General, the Departments of Political Affairs and of Peace-keeping Operations, the High Commissioner for Human Rights, and the United Nations Security Coordinator;
- Governments, including both countries affected by emergencies and donor countries;
- Relevant intergovernmental bodies, particularly the Security Council and the General Assembly;
- The international media; and
- A wide range of public groups.

Maintaining ties with this array of actors is a challenging task. While it is done in many ways, within the United Nations system there are two main approaches: coordinating the humanitarian community through the Inter-Agency Standing Committee (IASC); and linking the humanitarian community to the political and security components of the United Nations.

Coordination within the humanitarian community. IASC, chaired by the ERC, is the primary forum for coordinating the international humanitarian response to emergencies. Established by General Assembly resolution 46/182, the primary tasks of IASC include:

- Setting policies for the United Nations humanitarian system on such issues as providing assistance and protection to internally displaced persons (IDPs), linking relief and development, and strengthening system-wide accountability, monitoring and evaluation;
- Allocating responsibilities among participating entities in particular crises; and
- Addressing major policies and operational decisions relating to particular humanitarian crises.

Permanent IASC members include FAO, UNDP, UNHCR, UNICEF, WFP and WHO (see box opposite). Standing invitations are extended to IOM, the ICRC, the IFRC, three consortia of non-governmental organizations—Inter-Action, the International Council of Voluntary Agencies (ICVA) and the Steering Committee for Humanitarian Response (SCHR)—and, as of

early 1997, the United Nations High Commissioner for Human Rights. Other organizations, including the International Bank for Reconstruction and Development (World Bank) and the Representative of the Secretary-General on IDPs, are invited on an ad hoc basis.

IASC meets several times a year at the level of heads of agency. Its Working Group, however, meets bimonthly or more frequently, if necessary, to address more immediate issues, and to prepare policy and other recommendations for the heads of agencies. It also uses specific task forces to work on given policy issues. Weekly inter-agency meetings in both New York and Geneva exchange country-specific information and time-sensitive updates. Other consultations among IASC members take place frequently—from the heads of agency down to the staff level—and almost constantly when an emergency is acute. In spring 1997 DHA, working very closely with IASC, is preparing the report of the Secretary-General to the United Nations Economic and Social Council (ECOSOC) on strengthening the capacity of the United Nations humanitarian system, called for by Council resolution 95/56.

Coordination with the rest of the United Nations. The second main approach to coordination involves cooperation between the humanitarian community and those parts of the United Nations that do not have explicit humanitarian responsibilities, but whose work bears significantly upon humanitarian affairs. Cooperation with a number of such entities has been markedly strengthened in the past several years.

Cooperation between DHA and other parts of the Secretariat has become well established. As part of the ''Framework for Cooperation'', senior staff of the Department of Political Affairs, the Department of Peace-keeping Operations and DHA have met on a regular basis since 1993 to share information on countries in crisis. In addition, working meetings between the three Departments review these situations and propose ways for the United Nations to address the problem.

At the intergovernmental level, DHA and United Nations humanitar-

The Disaster Management Training Programme

The Crisis Environments Training Initiative

Initiated in 1990 as a key element of the International Decade for Natural Disaster Reduction, the joint DHA/UNDP Disaster Management Training Programme (DMTP) does system-wide management training and capacity-building for both natural disasters and complex emergencies. The Programme supports training both in disaster preparedness and mitigation and in emergency response, so as to reduce vulnerabilities to disasters and emergencies and to create conditions favourable to sustainable development.

Over the past seven years, DMTP has :

- generated methodologies and materials for emergency/disaster management training, including: training modules with companion trainers' guides; case-studies; simulation exercises; videos, and training guidelines;
- helped train managers at the national level in countries impacted by disasters and emergencies;
- conducted three training-of-trainers events for 55 United Nations inter-agency trainers from UNICEF, DHA, UNDP, WFP, UNHCR, FAO and WHO; and
- strengthened networking and improved coordination between international partners involved in humanitarian assistance.

DMTP has held regional or country-level workshops in 65 countries in Africa, Latin America and the Caribbean, the Middle East, Asia and the former Soviet Union. They have trained 4,000-5,000 participants, including: country officials (50 per cent), United Nations staff (20 per cent), NGO staff (20 per cent) and officials of donor Governments (10 per cent). Most of the training modules are available in English, French and Spanish and selected ones have been translated into Arabic, Bahasa Indonesian, Chinese, Farsi, Portuguese, Russian and Vietnamese.

In the future, DMTP will:

- introduce the Country Capacity-Building Programme to increase preparedness in selected countries through such initiatives as disaster manager training, hazard mapping, and improving disaster response planning;
- encourage United Nations and other international institutions to integrate disaster and emergency management into overall programmes; and
- expand the DMTP Steering Committee so as to include additional United Nations agencies such as UNEP, UNESCO, WMO and Habitat.

On the recommendation of IASC in 1995, DHA established a new unit within DMTP: the Crisis Environments Training Initiative (CETI). This initiative addresses the special training requirements of United Nations agencies and NGOs working in complex humanitarian emergencies. Since that time, seven consultations have been held with IASC members to:

- identify important issues on which additional training is needed;
- develop strategies appropriate for each agency's specific mandate; and
- implement training in both the field and at headquarters to strengthen coordination and delivery of humanitarian assistance.

In February 1997, the first CETI training module was published, entitled *Coordination Among International Organizations in Complex Emergencies*. Modules currently under development include: Contingency Planning; Joint Assessment and the Consolidated Appeals Process; Humanitarian Principles; International Humanitarian Law and (together with DMTP), Conflict Transformation and Media Relations. IASC has also requested CETI to develop training modules on internally displaced persons (IDPs) and on the management of emergency response personnel. Additional topics and strategies for inter-agency delivery of training are currently under discussion.

DHA is now preparing an inventory of all training materials and activities within the United Nations system relevant to humanitarian assistance. This data will be placed on ReliefWeb and will be regularly updated to provide readily available information, searchable by agency or by key word, about training resources and opportunities (see annex II, page 108).

manitarian agencies present in the affected country and may be expanded to include others as appropriate.

For sudden-onset disasters, DHA is normally represented by the United Nations Resident Coordinator in the country in question. In a natural disaster, the Government in most instances would request international support and the United Nations Resident Coordinator and UNDMT would assist the Government's relief and coordination efforts. Most often this entails working at the interface between the national and international assistance systems: helping to obtain, analyse, and disseminate information about relief needs and actions; and deploying international specialists in relief coordination to help manage the wave of outside assistance at the relief site. DHA headquarters in Geneva ensures that the needed stand-by capacities and services are rapidly deployed, organizes needs assessments and mobilizes resources.

The United Nations Resident Coordinator typically represents DHA in the early warning and initial response phases of a humanitarian emergency. When a situation threatens to become a full-blown crisis, the ERC, in consultation with IASC, reviews the profile of this individual to ensure that he/she has the necessary experience and skills. If so, the Resident Coordinator is confirmed as the United Nations Humanitarian Coordinator for the emergency; if not, another individual with the required "profile" will be appointed as Humanitarian Coordinator.

In complex emergencies, the Humanitarian Coordinator must cooperate with a wide range of actors, in addition to the humanitarian organizations. In most cases it is crucial to deal, not only with the Government of the affected country, but also with the main opposition groups, in order to obtain access to those in need in areas the contending parties control. Major donor Governments are also often present in the country, as well as numerous international NGOs delivering assistance. There may also be a peace-keeping mission, whether under the auspices of the United Nations, a regional organization or a multinational force; a Special Representative or Special Envoy of the

ian agencies frequently report to the Security Council when it considers issues with significant humanitarian implications. In addition to these regular appearances at the Council, DHA recently organized presentations to the Council and other Member States by three humanitarian NGOs—Médecins sans frontières, Care International and OXFAM—concerning obstacles to gaining access to refugees in need of assistance in eastern Zaire. The willingness of Security Council members to consider such viewpoints is crucial to ensuring that their decisions take full cognizance of humanitarian concerns and consequences.

Coordination in the field

As noted earlier, emergencies which fall within the mandate and capacity of a single United Nations agency do not require active DHA involvement. A recent example was the WHO response to the outbreak of the Ebola

virus in central Africa. There are also situations in which most, but not all the United Nations assistance required can be provided by a particular United Nations agency. In such circumstances, the Emergency Relief Coordinator, in consultation with IASC, may designate a lead agency to coordinate the United Nations response. However, most emergencies requiring United Nations humanitarian involvement call for significant participation by a number of United Nations agencies. In these cases, the ERC would, in consultation with IASC, appoint a Humanitarian Coordinator to ensure effective coordination of United Nations humanitarian efforts.

The Humanitarian Coordinator. Parallel to the roles of the ERC and IASC at the headquarters level, the Humanitarian Coordinator works closely in the field with the United Nations Disaster Management Team (UNDMT), which includes representatives of the United Nations hu-

United Nations Secretary-General; and other special negotiators representing regional organizations or important countries. Lastly, security issues are especially critical for humanitarian staff and operations, and the United Nations Designated Official for Security in-country is a key partner.

In the United Nations system of humanitarian coordination, a distinction is made between operational coordination, which is undertaken by the United Nations agencies themselves, and strategic coordination, which is the responsibility of DHA.

Operational coordination. Occurs where the United Nations humanitarian agencies have standing mandates, designated areas of responsibility and ongoing operations. In such cases, one or other of these agencies may play a coordination role within its particular area of expertise. UNICEF, for example, often takes the lead in water and sanitation programmes within the larger inter-agency coordination process, as does UNHCR where the problem is predominantly or exclusively related to refugees. There have also been recent examples of a particular agency providing common services to other United Nations agencies, as well as to the wider humanitarian community. WFP, for example, has sometimes taken responsibility for transport and logistics on behalf of others. DHA is responsible for ensuring that such operational coordination is carried out effectively.

Strategic coordination. Addresses the overall conditions required for humanitarian assistance efforts to succeed. A fairly extensive listing of such functions in the IASC-approved Terms of Reference of the Humanitarian Coordinator, includes:

- developing coordinated approaches to strategic planning, situation and needs assessment, and resource mobilization;
- negotiating access to those in need;
- negotiating with relevant authorities about overall policies and procedures for relief efforts;
- allocating responsibilities among humanitarian entities; and
- producing and disseminating important information about humanitarian needs and the actions and resources required to meet them.

Support for DHA field coordination. In order for coordination to be effective, the Humanitarian Coordinator needs timely support. At the field level, this includes the provision of adequate numbers of qualified staff, and the necessary financial, logistical, and other support to allow them to function. Strengthening such support to the field has been a top priority for DHA in the past several years. Two types of support are particularly important.

Coordination Units. In small or short-term complex emergencies, providing one or two DHA staff on mission to the field may be all the extra personnel the Humanitarian Coordinator requires. However, for most complex emergencies, longer-term staff are needed, organized into a Field Coordination Unit. DHA currently has 15 such units in particular countries, as well as three units with regional mandates: one for the Great Lakes Region, the Integrated Regional Information Network in Nairobi, and a West Africa Regional Focal Point in Abidjan. (See map I, pages 4 and 5, and annex I, page 107.)

Depending on the local circumstances, these Field Coordination Units can range from a few people, in the case of Sierra Leone, to larger ones, such as in Angola and Afghanistan. (See box, pages 16 and 17.) The staff for such units is typically drawn from several sources, principally from United Nations humanitarian agencies, but often from NGOs or donor Governments. However, most of the staff usually come from DHA itself, or through one of its stand-by support mechanisms.

Mechanisms and services for field support. While some mechanisms and services are specifically designed for natural disasters or for complex emergencies, most can be used in either type of humanitarian crisis. Examples include:

- *Rapid deployment of internal staff.* DHA deploys experienced headquarters staff to the field on short notice. The Rapid Response Roster is used to provide pre-screened external personnel who are then placed on DHA contracts for field deployment in a particular emergency.

- *Stand-by mechanisms for deployment of external staff.* The United Nations Disaster Assessment and Coordination Team (UNDAC) mechanism provides experienced relief experts from Europe and Latin America. Supported by their national emergency agency, they are available for deployment to the field in a matter of hours in sudden-onset or natural disasters or within days in complex emergencies. Experienced staff are also provided on short notice via stand-by arrangements with the Norwegian and Danish Refugee Councils, often funded by their respective Governments.

- *Stand-by logistics support.* Stand-by stocks of key logistical support items, such as telecommunications equipment, specially equipped field vehicles, and personal support kits, together with stand-by specialist staff to help install and maintain this equipment, are provided via the Swedish Rescue Services Agency (SRSA), the Danish Emergency Management Agency (DEMA) and the Emergency Logistics Unit of the United Kingdom (ODA). DHA also maintains in Geneva limited stocks of certain key equipment and supplies such as satellite telecommunications sets and administrative support kits.

- *The Pisa Warehouse.* DHA, in cooperation with WHO, WFP, and the Governments of Italy, Japan, Luxembourg and Norway, maintains stocks of about 20 relief items in its warehouse in Pisa, Italy. Supplies can be dispatched to the field either as a bilateral donation, or through the United Nations, on behalf of WHO or WFP, or at the request of the United Nations Disaster Management Team to help fill critical relief gaps.

- *The Military and Civil Defence Unit (MCDU).* Established through an inter-agency agreement in 1996, MCDU facilitates the use of appropriate military or civil defence resources by United

Coordination structure in Sierra Leone

Of all of Africa's current disturbances, Sierra Leone's is one of the most overlooked. Often cited as a "silent emergency", at the height of the crisis, over 40 per cent of its pre-war population was displaced. In 1995, the situation in Sierra Leone had deteriorated, the conflict spreading in the north and west of the country, and insurgents advancing within 20 kilometres of Freetown. Population movements, levels of security and access to beneficiaries changed frequently, necessitating stronger coordination of an increasing number of organizations undertaking relief interventions. IASC dispatched a mission to Sierra Leone which resulted in the appointment of a United Nations Humanitarian Coordinator and the establishment of the United Nations Humanitarian Assistance Coordination Unit (UN-HACU) in Freetown.

Making a difference

UN-HACU fostered a network of committees organized by sectors, such as health, agriculture, water and sanitation, which meet regularly, bringing together United Nations agencies, the Government, donors, NGOs and the local community (see chart on inter-agency meetings below). This enabled the humanitarian community to identify gaps and priorities for interventions, enhancing the cohesiveness and efficiency of emergency response. As a result, the humanitarian community as a whole began to exchange ideas and share resources to ensure as complete a coverage as possible. UN-HACU also included local NGOs in planning. An umbrella organization for local NGOs, the National NGO Forum, was conceived in meetings prompted by UN-HACU.

> *"DHA fulfils a vital function and provides a critical service by improving coordination of the humanitarian response during a complex emergency."*
>
> United Nations Office of Internal Oversight Services, upon review of UN-HACU Sierra Leone in 1996.

Coordination in action: UN-HACU activities and their impact

Providing a focal point

- Provided a field link for policy coordination and information-sharing among the political, military, humanitarian and development actors of the United Nations system.
- Established offices at front-line areas in Bo, Kenema, and Makeni, where population movement was most fluid.

HUMANITARIAN COORDINATION ACTION
Regular inter-agency emergency-related meeting in Freetown, Sierra Leone
August 1996

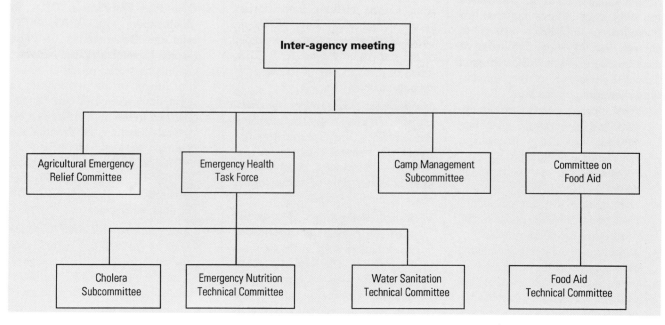

- Provided material, technical, and personnel support to the Ministry of National Reconstruction, Resettlement and Rehabilitation (MNRRR) in establishing provincial offices for humanitarian coordination. This facilitated decentralized coordination and sharing of information and other resources.
- UN-HACU premises were available for use by humanitarian partners to convene meetings and to share information through an efficient mail drop system.

Situation analysis/information-sharing

- Served as a clearing-house for information on humanitarian activities:
  - produced/disseminated situation reports;
  - provided informal briefings and advice to new arrivals and assessment missions;
  - maintained a chart of NGO activities to help identify areas lacking assistance;
  - maintained a register of security incidents and provided briefs and analyses;
  - supported the establishment and operation of the Sierra Leone Integrated Information Centre (SLIIC), a central information registry maintained by the humanitarian community in Sierra Leone.
- Organized integrated assessment missions to "pockets" of crisis to get an accurate picture, thereby improving programme targeting. Developed "rapid assessment forms" for overall analyses.
- UN-HACU's database provided the most accurate population information available, including family profiles, nutritional surveys, agricultural assessments, as well as assessment mission and registration/verification results. It is being merged with SLIIC.

> *"Through its transparent and collaborative approach, UN-HACU has played an effective role among United Nations agencies, Government, NGOs and donors. UNHCR has particularly benefited from UN-HACU's role as an information focal point; the UN-HACU database has helped us plan the reintegration component of our repatriation programme."*
>
> Akilaja Akiwumi, UNHCR
> Country Representative

Bridging gaps

- UN-HACU, perceived as a neutral coordinating body, coordinated relocation of groups of internally displaced persons crammed in Kissy Dockyard: a task which was not covered by the mandate of any United Nations operational agency.
- In July 1996, 600 people from 17 agencies and organizations, organized by UN-HACU, registered displaced people in Bo. Similar exercises took place in Kenema, Freetown, allowing for:
  - strategic use of limited resources;
  - targeted assistance to vulnerable groups; and
  - creative use of food aid to encourage resettlement.
- In October 1996, when violent clashes occurred in Bo, UN-HACU acted as the interlocutor between the United Nations Security Officer and NGOs in relocating international staff to Freetown.

> *"UN-HACU has provided an effective co-ordination vehicle for tackling obstacles to the efficient delivery of emergency aid, problems that cannot be solved by any one agency in isolation."*
>
> Kristen Richardson, CRS
> Country Representative

Resource mobilization

- Consolidated inter-agency appeals in Sierra Leone involve extensive collaboration and include project proposals by local and international NGOs. A donor Government official commented, *"with the increase of actors in need of funds, we can no longer cope with the number of ad hoc requests coming from hundreds of NGOs, and are looking towards funding mostly those NGO projects which are a part of a larger, comprehensive, strategic plan, such as those coordinated by DHA through its Appeals"*.
- DHA utilized its various stand-by arrangements with the Swedish Rescue Services Agency (SRSA), the Norwegian Refugee Council (NRC) and the DHA Rapid Response Roster to ensure experienced emergency staff. UN-HACU was the first DHA office to utilize NRC's innovative African Stand-by Roster.

Nations agencies or other humanitarian organizations in need of them.

- **Emergency Funding.** The Central Emergency Revolving Fund (CERF), established with US$ 50 million in donor funding and managed by DHA, provides United Nations agencies with an emergency reserve upon which they can draw to cover funding shortfalls. DHA itself can draw on the interest on the CERF on the same basis for its emergency response needs pertaining to co-ordination arrangements. DHA can also provide small cash grants in the immediate aftermath of a natural disaster for the United Nations Resident Coordinator to utilize in order to fill urgent gaps, usually though the purchase of locally available items ■

FIGURE 3. *The tinged red hair indicative of malnutrition is evident on this young boy in Chongjin, DPRK.* [WFP/Tun Myatt]

Chapter 2

Resource mobilization

The success of the international community in addressing a humanitarian crisis depends not only on the formulation of a well-coordinated response, but also on raising the resources needed to ensure timely assistance. Given finite donor support, resources must be targeted to meet priorities within a broad strategic framework that sets clear goals for the humanitarian programme. Over the past few years, the variety and scope of mechanisms for funding humanitarian assistance programmes, and in particular, rapid response to crises, have increased.

Fund-raising for complex emergencies

In December 1991, General Assembly resolution 46/182 established two financial mechanisms—the Central Emergency Revolving Fund (CERF) and the Consolidated Appeal Process (CAP) to help DHA coordinate fund-raising from the international community in response to specific complex emergencies.

The Central Emergency Revolving Fund (CERF)

CERF is a cash-flow mechanism, under the authority of the ERC, to enable an immediate response to an emergency. CERF has been used at the very outset of an emergency and, in exceptional cases, during later phases to assist agencies with cash-flow problems before donor contributions are available. The mechanism requires that agencies borrowing from the fund reimburse the amount loaned within a specific target period, not to exceed one year. Figure 4 summarizes contributions totalling US$ 49,249,000 that have been made by donor Governments since the Fund's inception.

CERF has been used 48 times, with a total of US$ 124 million disbursed from April 1992 to December 1996. UNICEF, UNHCR and WFP account for 80 per cent of this total (see figure 5).

The amounts disbursed in any one year have fallen from US$ 48.6 million in 1993 to US$ 4 million in 1996 (see figure 6). This reduction in the use of CERF since 1993 appears to be the result of several factors:

- While many earlier humanitarian crises have continued, making borrowing from CERF difficult, no major new humanitarian emergencies have occurred, with the exception of the Great Lakes Region. This has reduced new borrowing from CERF;
- In the past few years, United Nations agencies have developed their own emergency funds for response: for example, the UNHCR Emergency Fund; the WFP International Emergency Food Reserve and Immediate Response Account; and the UNICEF Emergency Programme Fund. This trend has been encouraged by the ERC and DHA;
- Agencies have been constrained from using CERF, since they must repay the loans from the Fund and may be uncertain that donors will provide resources to allow repayment of a loan.

In general, CERF has proved useful in a number of emergencies—particularly in the Great Lakes, Horn of Africa and Iraq—where new or ongoing relief programmes of WFP, UNICEF and UNHCR would have been jeopardized without immediate funds. In Tajikistan, UNHCR was able to use CERF to meet a temporary shortfall in funding for a critical shelter programme, which allowed refugees to return without delay and on schedule.

Given the declining use of CERF over the past two years, however, the ongoing review of humanitarian coordination called for by ECOSOC resolution 1995/56 has elicited several proposals to expand the uses of CERF. One current proposal would create a "second window": providing funds for priority requirements for which donor funding might be uncertain and which need not be repaid if funding were not raised. There has been some reluctance among donor countries to support this proposal. Another proposal that is receiving support within IASC would permit access to CERF by those non-governmental organizations that have participated in the development of consolidated humanitarian programmes and that are included in the relevant Consolidated Inter-Agency Appeal. Further review at the July 1997 session of ECOSOC in Geneva will determine how CERF might best play a role in the overall resource mobilization strategy for new and ongoing complex emergencies.

The Consolidated Inter-Agency Appeal Process (CAP)

From 1992-1996, 68 Consolidated Inter-Agency Appeals were launched by DHA. A total of US$ 14.2 billion was sought through CAPs, of which approximately US$ 10.4 billion was raised, or 73 per cent of requirements (see figure 7). The largest number of Consolidated Appeals issued was 21, and the largest amount sought in a single year was nearly US$ 4 billion: both in 1993. The 1993 Appeal for the Former Yugoslavia alone sought almost US$ 1 billion. The total numbers of appeals as well as the total requirements have fallen since 1993, levelling off at 12-14 appeals seeking approximately US$ 2.35 billion in 1995 and 1996. In the past two years, the shortfall in contributions received increased from 20 per cent of the amount requested in 1995 to 32 per cent in 1996.

The breakdown of requirements and contributions by region shows that the largest requirements and number of emergencies are found in Africa where, in 1993 alone, ten

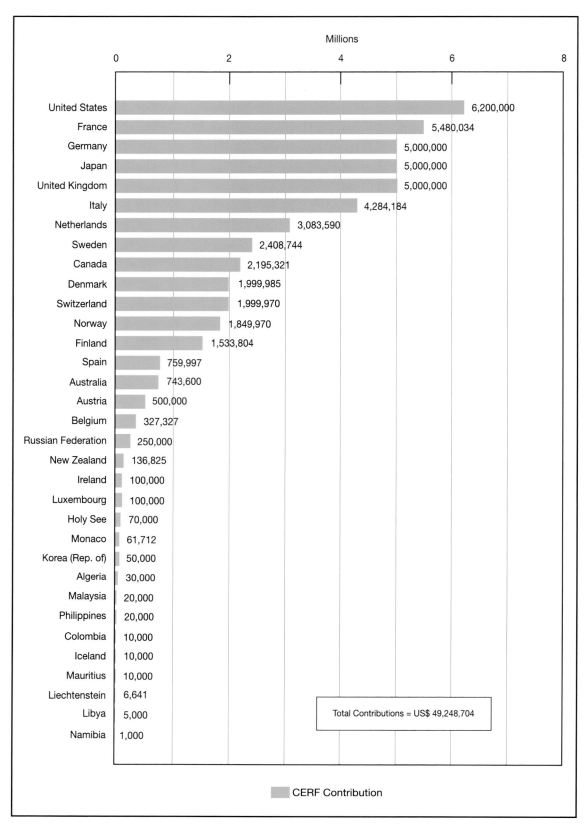

FIGURE 4. *1992-1996 Central Emergency Revolving Fund (CERF): status of contributions, by donor (value in US dollars).*

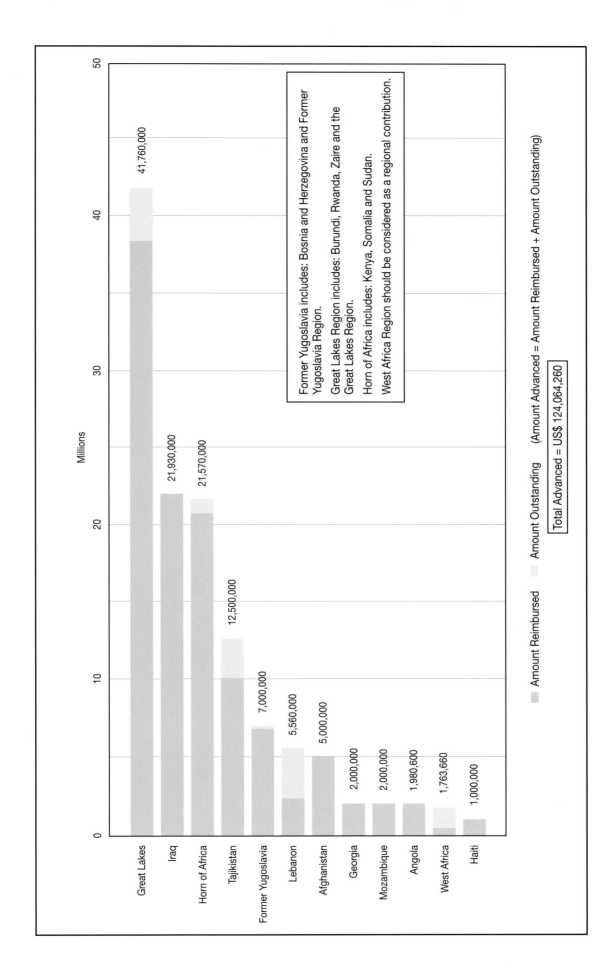

FIGURE 5. *1992-1996 CERF advances and reimbursements, by emergency (value in US dollars).*

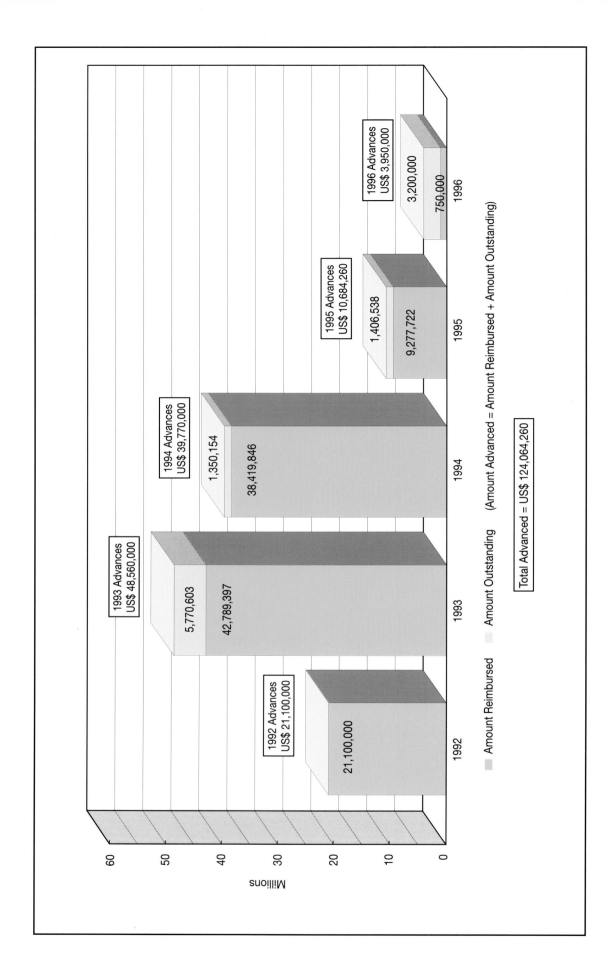

FIGURE 6. *1992-1996 Central Emergency Revolving Fund (CERF): consolidated advances and reimbursements (value in US dollars)*. .

22

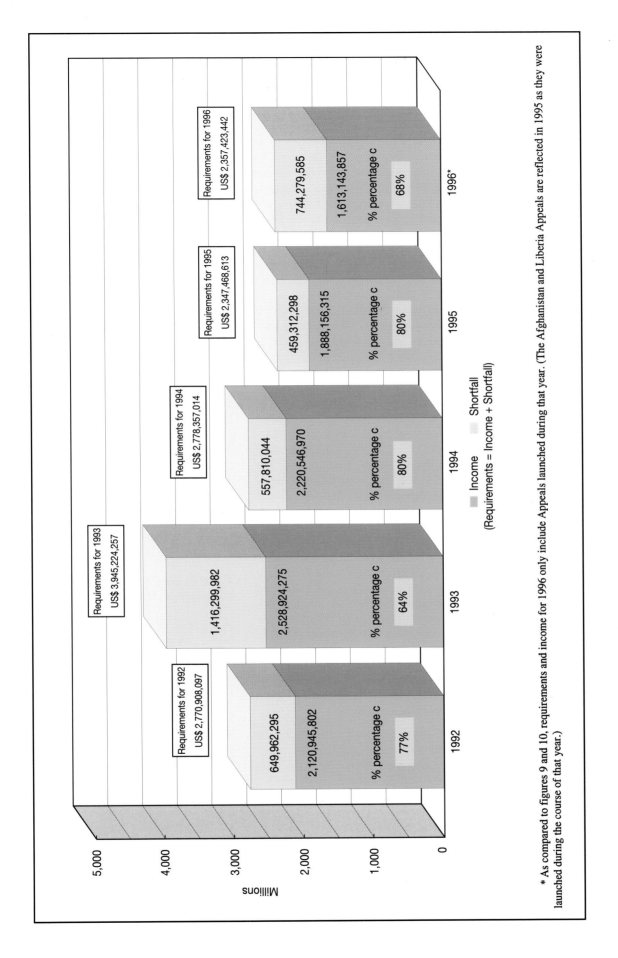

FIGURE 7. *United Nations Consolidated Inter-Agency Humanitarian Assistance Appeals: requirements and income from 1992-1996 (value in US dollars).*

* As compared to figures 9 and 10, requirements and income for 1996 only include Appeals launched during that year. (The Afghanistan and Liberia Appeals are reflected in 1995 as they were launched during the course of that year.)

Consolidated Appeals for countries or regions seeking US$ 2.1 billion were issued. In 1996, the number had fallen to six appeals for Africa, seeking US$ 1.2 billion, with the needs of the Great Lakes Region and Angola dominating. Since the establishment of DHA, the conflict and subsequent rehabilitation in the former Yugoslavia accounted for most of the funds required in Europe, while the humanitarian programmes in Iraq and Afghanistan accounted for the largest funding requirements in the Middle East and Asia, respectively (see figure 8).

Almost three quarters of the funds raised through the Consolidated Appeals process in 1996 were directed towards two emergencies: those in the Great Lakes Region and in former Yugoslavia, with the remaining 27 per cent contributing to the other 12 appeals. Several of the appeals which attracted relatively little donor support are long-standing ones which appear resistant to political settlement (see figure 9).

During the past five years, a few donors have provided the vast majority of contributions to the appeals. In 1996, the six largest donors were the United States, the European Union, Japan, the Netherlands, Sweden and the United Kingdom, accounting for approximately 64 per cent of all assistance (see figure 10).

The process of planning, preparing and tracking contributions to the CAPs has evolved considerably since 1992, consistent with the guidance of the IASC, its working group and numerous geographic task forces. At first, preparation of the CAP was not much more than a consolidation of individual agency and sectoral projects. Even at that stage, however, the CAP improved upon the prior practice of each agency producing its own appeal, with little or no consultation. The CAP is intended to provide donors with a consolidated proposal which minimizes overlaps and reflects inter-agency priorities among the full range of humanitarian needs in a given emergency.

As the Consolidated Appeals process has evolved, it has become not only the preparation of a fund-raising document, but also an instrument for coordination, consisting of four elements:

- Needs assessment;
- Strategic planning;
- Preparation of the appeal;
- Post-appeal follow-up and monitoring.

The Humanitarian Coordinator in the field takes the lead in the needs assessment process and involves not only the United Nations agencies, but also, where possible, other international organizations, donor Governments and NGOs. While not delaying a timely response to an immediate crisis, the assessment mission also develops a strategic plan which sets out, for all humanitarian partners in the field, a clear set of priority objectives, sectoral responsibilities and coordination arrangements. Wherever possible, the strategic plan also draws clear links between relief activities and reconstruction, rehabilitation and development activities carried out by development agencies such as UNDP, UNICEF, WFP, FAO and eventually the World Bank. Finally, once the appeal has been issued, DHA undertakes post-appeal follow-up and monitoring, by tracking and reporting on donor contributions. The Department issues monthly updates of contributions to all emergency operations, with detailed and summary financial information, including on the Internet through ReliefWeb (www.reliefweb.int). Tracking of contributions has been expanded to include contributions not only to the agencies included in the CAP, but also to other international organizations and NGOs, including direct bilateral contributions.

Given the time constraints in some very rapidly developing complex emergencies—such as the sudden flows of refugees from eastern Zaire back to Rwanda in late 1996—DHA sometimes issues ''Flash'' or Interim Appeals. These are prepared over the course of a few weeks and usually cover emergency requirements for only a few months. During this period, a more comprehensive effort is undertaken to produce a follow-on CAP: incorporating the requirements presented in the Flash Appeal, together with more detailed needs assessment and strategic planning components.

The future of the CAP

While the CAP process has come a long way since its inception, improvements are still needed. Delays in the production of appeals can occur, particularly when the emergency involves several countries, and these delays can create planning and coordination problems. Moreover, in the early stages of an emergency, it is sometimes difficult to involve all relevant international, national and local actors and to prioritize a comprehensive range of relief and recovery requirements as part of an overall strategic plan. Yet only if such priorities and linkages are included can the CAP serve as the principal means of conveying the information donors require if they are to confidently commit funds in complex emergencies. The CAP, which is a flexible mechanism and can be adjusted as additional experience is gained, is likely to remain the primary means to direct efficient, timely and appropriate humanitarian assistance to those affected by complex emergencies. In response to ECOSOC resolution 1995/56, recommendations to strengthen the CAP mechanism will be presented at its substantive session in July 1997.

Fund-raising for natural and technological disasters

In contrast to complex emergencies which can evolve over time and persist for many years, natural or technological disasters tend to happen suddenly. Thus disasters require an urgent response, but one that is quite specific and, usually, of fairly limited duration. When a country suffers such a sudden-onset disaster and seeks international assistance, DHA takes the lead within the United Nations system in mobilizing the required resources, be they cash, in kind or services.

Through DHA situation reports, appeals with specific emergency relief requirements are disseminated instantaneously to more than 700 potential donors and relevant international partners through an e-mail distribution system, as well as to the public at large through the Internet (www.reliefweb.int/dha_ol). These situation reports serve as an impor-

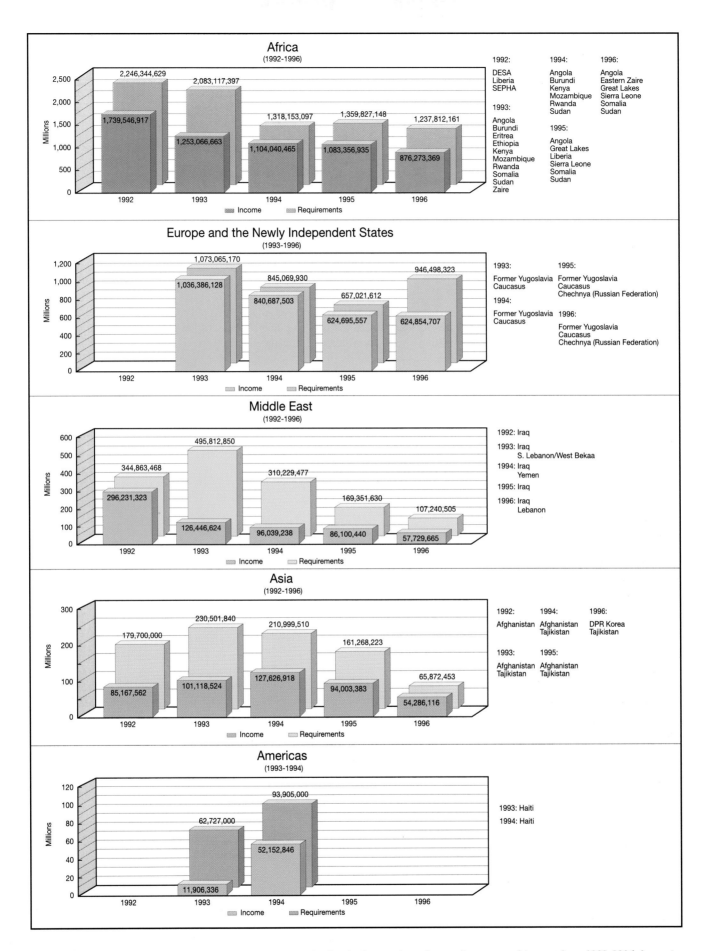

FIGURE 8. *United Nations Consolidated Inter-Agency Humanitarian Assistance Appeals: requirements and income from 1992-1996, by region (value in US dollars).*

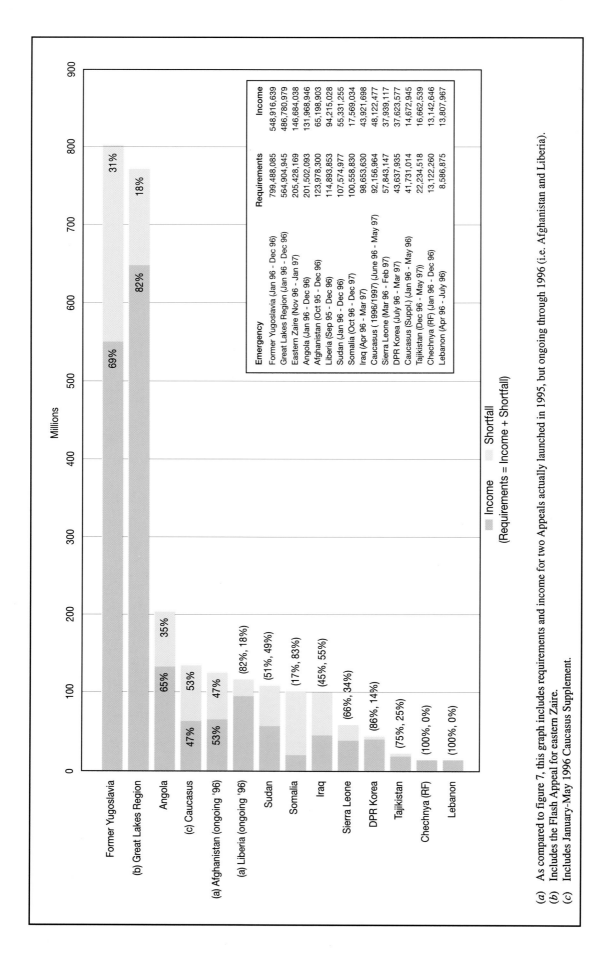

FIGURE 9. *United Nations Consolidated Inter-Agency Humanitarian Assistance Appeals: requirements and income for Appeal launched/ongoing in 1996 (a) (value in US dollars).*

(*a*)   As compared to figure 7, this graph includes requirements and income for two Appeals actually launched in 1995, but ongoing through 1996 (i.e. Afghanistan and Liberia).
(*b*)   Includes the Flash Appeal for eastern Zaire.
(*c*)   Includes January-May 1996 Caucasus Supplement.

Emergency	Requirements	Income
Former Yugoslavia (Jan 96 - Dec 96)	799,488,085	548,916,639
Great Lakes Region (Jan 96 - Dec 96)	564,904,945	486,780,979
Eastern Zaire (Nov 96 - Jan 97)	205,428,169	146,684,038
Angola (Jan 96 - Dec 96)	201,502,093	131,968,946
Afghanistan (Oct 95 - Dec 96)	123,978,300	65,198,903
Liberia (Sep 95 - Dec 96)	114,893,853	94,215,028
Sudan (Jan 96 - Dec 96)	107,574,977	55,331,255
Somalia (Oct 96 - Dec 97)	100,558,830	17,569,034
Iraq (Apr 96 - Mar 97)	98,653,630	43,921,698
Caucasus (1996/1997) (June 96 - May 97)	92,156,964	48,122,477
Sierra Leone (Mar 96 - Feb 97)	57,843,147	37,939,117
DPR Korea (July 96 - Mar 97)	43,637,935	37,623,577
Caucasus (Suppl.) (Jan 96 - May 96)	41,731,014	14,672,945
Tajikistan (Dec 96 - May 97)	22,234,518	16,662,539
Chechnya (RF) (Jan 96 - Dec 96)	13,122,260	13,142,646
Lebanon (Apr 96 - July 96)	8,586,875	13,807,967

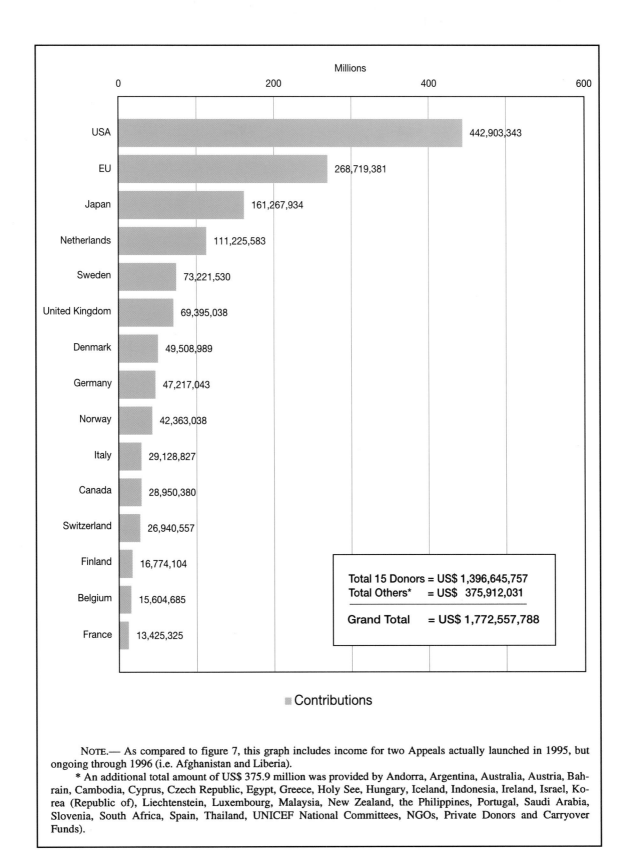

Millions

USA	442,903,343
EU	268,719,381
Japan	161,267,934
Netherlands	111,225,583
Sweden	73,221,530
United Kingdom	69,395,038
Denmark	49,508,989
Germany	47,217,043
Norway	42,363,038
Italy	29,128,827
Canada	28,950,380
Switzerland	26,940,557
Finland	16,774,104
Belgium	15,604,685
France	13,425,325

Total 15 Donors = US$ 1,396,645,757
Total Others* = US$ 375,912,031
_____
Grand Total = US$ 1,772,557,788

■ Contributions

NOTE.— As compared to figure 7, this graph includes income for two Appeals actually launched in 1995, but ongoing through 1996 (i.e. Afghanistan and Liberia).

* An additional total amount of US$ 375.9 million was provided by Andorra, Argentina, Australia, Austria, Bahrain, Cambodia, Cyprus, Czech Republic, Egypt, Greece, Holy See, Hungary, Iceland, Indonesia, Ireland, Israel, Korea (Republic of), Liechtenstein, Luxembourg, Malaysia, New Zealand, the Philippines, Portugal, Saudi Arabia, Slovenia, South Africa, Spain, Thailand, UNICEF National Committees, NGOs, Private Donors and Carryover Funds).

FIGURE 10. *United Nations Consolidated Inter-Agency Humanitarian Assistance Appeals: contributions by the 15 major donors to Appeals launched/ongoing in 1996 (value in US dollars).*

tant means of influencing donors' decisions about whether and how to respond to the disaster. DHA also contacts national emergency relief services in donor countries and the emergency services of relief agencies to mobilize assistance and advise on the most appropriate type of aid.

In many disasters, cash resources for local or regional purchases are the most appropriate means of support. In these instances, DHA can immediately provide an emergency cash grant of up to US$ 50,000 for any one disaster, bridging the gap until supplementary donor funding becomes available. Over the past five years, DHA has provided emergency cash grants totalling an average of US$ 767,000 per year (see figure 11).

In addition, donors frequently choose to channel their funds through DHA to promote a coordinated response to the disaster. DHA has recently made arrangements with Italy and Norway to deposit funds in reserve in a Trust Fund for Disaster Relief for quick release in case of need. This reserve would be further strengthened should additional donors decide to participate. If provided the requisite information by donors, DHA also maintains records and issues reports on total funding provided to the affected country through channels other than DHA

Emergency aid as percentage of total overseas development expenditure[1] 1992-1995		
Year	Excluding food aid (per cent)	Including food aid (per cent)
1992	4.2	7.6
1993	5.7	8.7
1994	5.8	8.9
1995	5.2	7.5

[1] Internet address: http://www.oecd.org/dac/htm/table2.htm.

(see figure 12). The five largest government donors to sudden-onset disasters in 1996 were Italy, Norway, Luxembourg, the United Kingdom and Germany (see figure 13).

Future funding for humanitarian assistance

According to the 1996 report of the OECD Development Assistance Committee (DAC), total net overseas development assistance from DAC member countries, other donor countries, and multilateral organizations to developing countries and territories has remained at, or slightly below, US$ 60 billion per year between 1992 and 1995.

The table above gives expenditures on emergency aid by DAC member countries as a percentage of total Overseas Development Assistance (ODA). It shows that the percentage of ODA expended on emergency humanitarian assistance—both including and excluding food aid—peaked in 1994 and declined in 1995: the last year for which full data is available from DAC.

Given the flat level of ODA in current dollars over the past few years, this data suggests that the total amount of emergency aid seems to have peaked, and may well be declining. Some of the decline is of course explained by the slowly declining number of ongoing complex humanitarian emergencies. Another possible factor may be donor fatigue, particularly with long-standing humanitarian emergencies which appear resistant to political settlement ■

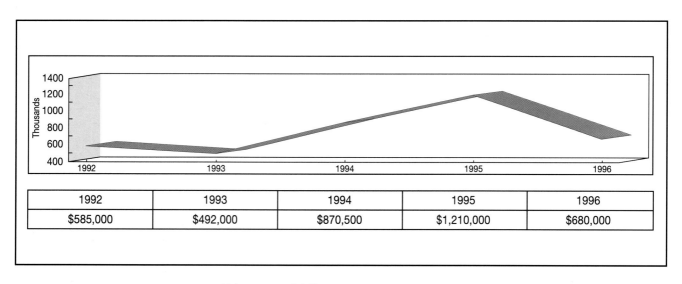

1992	1993	1994	1995	1996
$585,000	$492,000	$870,500	$1,210,000	$680,000

FIGURE 11. *DHA Emergency Grant, 1992-1996 (value in US dollars).*

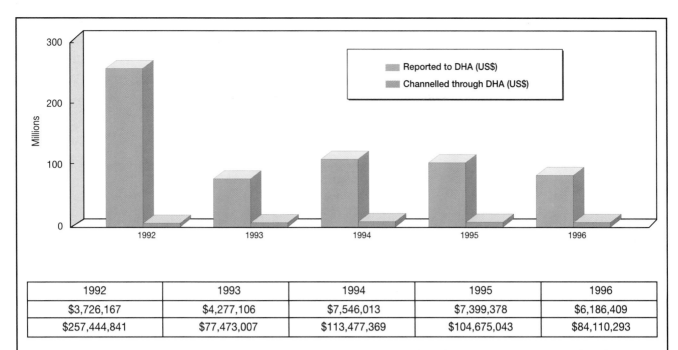

1992	1993	1994	1995	1996
$3,726,167	$4,277,106	$7,546,013	$7,399,378	$6,186,409
$257,444,841	$77,473,007	$113,477,369	$104,675,043	$84,110,293

* The figure of over US$ 257 million worth of contributions reported to DHA in 1992 was due to the exceptionally high international response, particularly by Arab countries, following the October 1992 earthquake in Egypt. The total amount of cash and in-kind contributions reported by donors in response to that disaster was in excess of US$ 193 million. The amount of other contributions reported in that year was comparable to amounts in subsequent years.

FIGURE 12. *Funding trends for sudden-onset disasters, 1992-1996 (value in US dollars).*

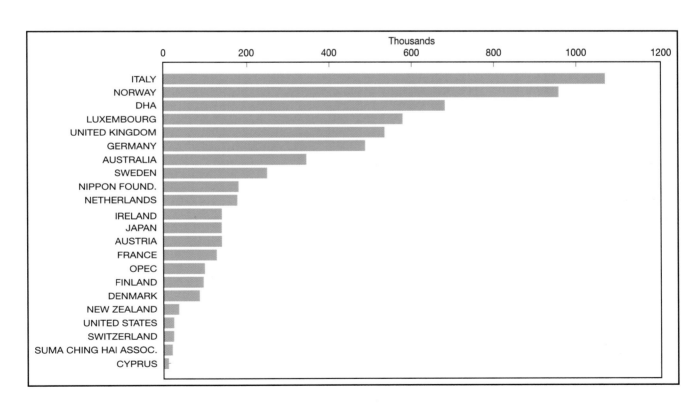

FIGURE 13. *Cash and in-kind contributions to sudden-onset disasters channelled through DHA in 1996, by donor (value in US dollars).*

Chapter 3

Information in humanitarian response

Existing and potential humanitarian crises are characterized by rapidly-changing conditions on the ground. Decisions on when, where, and how to respond must be made on the basis of the most up-to-date, accurate, and relevant information. Without it, well-intentioned humanitarian actions risk being ineffective, inefficient and, often, too late.

In early 1994, humanitarian agencies did not anticipate the speed and magnitude of the outflow of Rwandan refugees into neighbouring countries. That July, lacking critical information, relief organizations began working in eastern Zaire without appropriate supplies to cope with the spreading cholera epidemic. Later, aid providers were confronted with the need to protect and assist refugee populations that included many responsible for the genocide. Information alone would not have solved all the problems, but a system for information exchange would have improved both the coordination and the effectiveness of response.

Relevant information must reach decision makers, and decisions and other information must be relayed back to those implementing the response. At each stage of the crisis and the humanitarian response, there are distinct information needs. In order to initiate preventive or preparedness actions in anticipation of a crisis, decision makers require concise, analytic information on potential crises, worrisome developments and likely scenarios. In order to properly direct relief operations, programme officers must know what needs exist, what resources are required, and where to position supplies. In order to ensure that life-saving supplies reach victims of disasters, field workers require detailed operational and logistical information. Other situation-specific information is also critical for humanitarian organizations to ensure the security of their field workers and for donors who wish to use limited resources as effectively as possible.

General Assembly resolution 46/182 acknowledged the importance of information in ensuring a timely and effective response to crises by the United Nations system. The Emergency Relief Coordinator (ERC) was called upon to maintain ''an overview of all emergencies through, *inter alia*, the systematic pooling and analysis of early-warning information . . .'', and to provide ''consolidated information, including early warning on emergencies, to all interested Governments and concerned authorities, particularly affected and disaster prone countries, drawing on the capacities of the organizations of the system and other available sources''.

The DHA coordination role requires that it be able to keep decision makers and implementers in many different institutions informed as they respond to large emergencies. A common understanding of the scale of, and changes in, an ongoing emergency is critical in developing compatible strategies, so that organizations work together and not at cross purposes. Acting as a central information resource, DHA provides the knowledge base for a common understanding of what is needed for preparing for, and responding to, the humanitarian emergency as it unfolds.

In addition to traditional information channels at headquarters and in the field, DHA has developed three specific types of information initiatives (see figure 16, page 34). These are:

- *Early Warning System*: The Humanitarian Early Warning System (HEWS), established by DHA in 1993, generates background profiles, analytic briefs, and reports for United Nations decision makers, identifying potential crisis areas and recommending possible courses of action.

Humanitarian Early Warning System (HEWS)

- Analyses information on potential crises with humanitarian implications, focusing on existing vulnerabilities and developing trends
- Formulates scenarios and policy options
- Focuses on a small number of potential emergencies and reports to United Nations decision makers

- *Regional/country information networks*: In 1995, DHA established its first Integrated Regional Information Network (IRIN) to help manage the massive flow of information to and from the various actors engaged in the Great Lakes Region of Central Africa. This field orientation, which can focus on a country or region, increasingly characterizes other information networks, for example, in West Africa.

- *A global information platform*: In 1996, with the support of donor Governments and humanitarian NGOs, DHA developed ReliefWeb, a ''one-stop shopping'' platform on the Internet, providing information on complex emergencies and natural disasters from a wide variety of sources, including DHA, other United Nations agencies, NGOs, Governments, and the media.

Integrated Regional Information Network in the Great Lakes (IRIN-GL)

- Reports on developments in the region and assesses their implications for ongoing operations
- Synthesizes information from several and varied sources
- Publishes daily updates and periodic special reports targeted at United Nations headquarters, humanitarian agencies, governments, and operational NGOs

---

ReliefWeb

- Collects, organizes, and disseminates reports, maps, and logistical information from United Nations agencies, NGOs, Governments and the media
- Focuses on natural disasters and complex emergencies
- Updates provided twice daily on the Internet

While HEWS, ReliefWeb and the regional/country networks have discrete functions, in tandem they provide DHA and the humanitarian community with a shared information base on current and potential emergencies.

Early warning system

Man-made crises and natural disasters incur tremendous costs in terms of lives and scarce resources. More and more, the international community is called upon to anticipate these emergencies rather than acting only after they have broken out. Thus, in 1993, shortly after it was established, DHA set up the Humanitarian Early Warning System (HEWS) to identify potential crises with implications for the humanitarian community, in particular the United Nations. HEWS has developed extensive databases, including indicators of approaching tensions, assessments of existing vulnerabilities, trends and escalation potential. Using information from United Nations organizations, the Bretton Woods institutions, regional organizations, Member States, academia, NGOs, and some private sources, HEWS can generate background profiles, analytic briefs, and other reports on situations of concern.

HEWS focuses on country situations where latent or low-level tensions have not yet attracted significant attention but could escalate. It considers such general factors as prevailing socio-economic trends, the food supply, human rights violations, economic, social or political disparities between groups or regions, and the distribution and flow of arms. In cooperation with United Nations field offices and where possible, IRINs, HEWS has begun to develop indicators appropriate for monitoring a given country's situation, such as: the price of key export commodities; the price of basic food items; the rate of inflation; the level of livestock sales; or the number of months that public-sector employees, including soldiers, have not been paid. Its analyses recognize that several different factors can trigger a crisis and distinguish between root causes and triggering events.

Not an end unto itself, an early warning system should assist decision-making in order to spur preventive measures, where possible, and contingency planning, where necessary. Plans are under way for portions of HEWS information to be made available on ReliefWeb's Regional and Country Background section.

Regional/country information networks

Given the pace and multifaceted nature of many complex emergencies, United Nations agencies and other humanitarian partners must often struggle to gain a complete, accurate and current picture of a particular crisis as it evolves on the ground.

A regional model (IRINs):

In response to a critical need in the Great Lakes region of Central Africa, in November 1995 DHA established the Integrated Regional Information Network (IRIN-GL) in Nairobi. IRIN-GL provides timely information on the interrelated emergencies in the region, thus enabling operational United Nations agencies, NGOs and donors to monitor developments and respond more effectively. By introducing wire-service style updates, analyses and background briefings, IRIN-GL has revolutionized the United Nations' interactions with interested parties. By January 1997, IRIN-GL was producing daily updates for over one thousand primary subscribers in 42 countries.

IRIN-GL gathers and synthesizes information from a wide range of sources—national authorities, United Nations agencies, donor Governments, humanitarian NGOs, human rights organizations, political parties, regional institutions, academic institutions, and local and international media. To ensure a thorough picture, IRIN-GL collects public reports of the United Nations agencies and peace-keeping operations, other international organizations, OAU, the International Red Cross and Red Crescent Movement and NGOs, and makes them available either in response to specific enquiries or by subscription. In addition, IRIN-GL prepares thematic reports on specific issues, such as the situation in the Masisi area of eastern Zaire, or Uganda and the International Criminal Tribunal for Rwanda. IRIN-GL utilizes electronic mail and, as required, facsimiles, satellite phones, HF radio telex and hard-copy distribution. The information is also made available on ReliefWeb and is fed into HEWS. Given its regional expertise, IRIN-GL will work with HEWS to develop background information on other parts of the region.

Its proximity to agencies operating in the field enabled IRIN-GL to serve as a much-needed forum for information exchange as the crisis developed in eastern Zaire in late 1996. Having increased its reporting to twice daily in response to the crisis, IRIN-GL also introduced twice-weekly meetings which became an important regional focal point for information-sharing among the United Nations agencies, NGOs, donor representatives, and diplomats. These meetings continue to take place weekly in Nairobi and cover developments in the entire region.

The Great Lakes is only one region where complex political, social,

and military issues converge to create huge humanitarian needs and to complicate humanitarian response. The IRIN model is currently being replicated in West Africa. As of May 1997, IRIN-West Africa (IRIN-WA) in Abidjan will provide critical information and commentary on issues affecting humanitarian operations, initially in Liberia and Sierra Leone, where peace processes remain fragile and where renewed violence would have serious implications for operations throughout the entire region. Like IRIN-GL, IRIN-WA will improve the information flow, report regularly, monitor developments and special issues, and will track the implementation of United Nations Consolidated Inter-Agency Appeals. With HEWS, IRIN-WA will also strengthen DHA understanding of the countries throughout the region and assist HEWS in monitoring the latest developments. Like that of IRIN-GL, IRIN-WA reporting will be available on ReliefWeb.

A country model:

Information networks have also been developed to meet the need for consolidated information in a particular country. As one example, in 1996, DHA and several NGOs initiated AzerWeb, a country-based information network linking 40 relief NGOs in Azerbaijan. This information network, maintained in Baku by Save the Children/USA, seeks to fill gaps in communications and coordination among major relief agencies in Azerbaijan. The system links agencies via modem and provides a central bulletin board as well as elec-

tronic mail. As a central repository for sectoral and field reports and consolidated monthly reports, it allows for rapid exchange of information on the activities of the relief agencies, thus improving coordination between headquarters and field operations, as well as increasing circulation of information via Relief-Web.

A country-based approach is being used in Sierra Leone by two NGOs—Volunteers in Technical Assistance (VITA) and Response Net—with support from the World Bank, as well as in Ethiopia, through the UNDP Emergencies Unit for Ethiopia. While financial and other resources are not likely to be available for every affected country, it is certain that information centres would improve operational coordination. Strengthening the linkages between such country-based units and the other DHA information initiatives—ReliefWeb, HEWS, and the IRINs—is an important priority.

A global information platform

What of other complex humanitarian crises or disasters? ReliefWeb, the DHA global information dissemination platform, features information on all natural disasters and complex emergencies for which an international appeal or a CAP has been launched. ReliefWeb is located on the Internet at www.reliefweb.int and provides information access to the wider international community interested in humanitarian emergencies. With significant financial support from donor governments, ReliefWeb

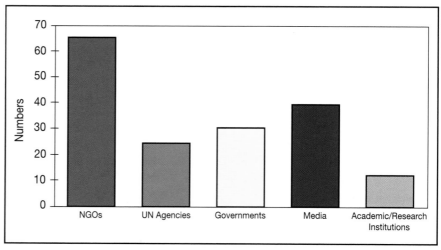

FIGURE 14. *Sources for ReliefWeb materials as of 8 March 1997.*

was officially launched at the World Aid Conference convened in Geneva in October 1996.

ReliefWeb consolidates and organizes information on current humanitarian emergencies from a network of 170 information sources, comprising 65 NGOs, 24 United Nations agencies and other international organizations, 30 governments and inter-governmental organizations, 39 media sources, and 12 academic institutions (see figure 14). Updated twice a day, five days a week, with emergency coverage on weekends, ReliefWeb features full-text documents of various types, maps, graphs charting contributions to appeals, logistical information for field operations, situation updates, and a background section covering seven regions that links to materials in other relevant web sites.

By including information from multiple sources, information can be compared, contrasted and even challenged. In mid-1996, ReliefWeb included reports produced by IRIN-GL, Amnesty International, Human Rights Watch, and the US Committee for Refugees on increasing tensions in eastern Zaire, several months prior to the outbreak of conflict in that area. During November and December 1996, daily coverage of population movements and assistance in the region helped the humanitarian community to visualize graphically the nature and extent of the humanitarian emergency and response.

ReliefWeb organizes this vast amount of information to avoid information overload. Documents on complex emergencies, for example, can be retrieved in four different ways:

- By date: documents are arranged chronologically;
- By source: documents are organized by source;
- By format: documents are categorized by type (appeal, evaluation, situation report); and
- By subject: using ReliefWeb's search engine, documents can be located by keyword descriptor or identifier.

Situation reports on natural disasters, such as those prepared by the United Nations Resident Coordinators, are

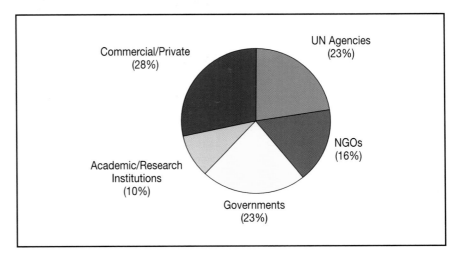

FIGURE 15. *ReliefWeb users as of 8 March 1997.*

also available. They include the latest facts on:

- the number of persons affected;
- the extent of damage; and
- the national and international response.

Alerts, dramatic news, and important announcements are also disseminated via e-mail directly to users who subscribe to the ReliefWeb Bulletin or who do not have Internet access.

ReliefWeb has formed information-sharing agreements with international organizations, Governments and NGOs. Its links to regional or country-based information networks, such as IRIN-Great Lakes and AzerWeb, significantly enhance the quality, timeliness, and relevance of reporting, while at the same time facilitating their dissemination to a much wider audience outside the country or region. Thus, ReliefWeb is beginning to serve as a global information-sharing platform for the international humanitarian community. Already, ReliefWeb attracts between 6,000 and 8,000 users on an average day. As figure 15 shows, current users include: United Nations agencies (23 per cent); NGOs (16 per cent); Governments (23 per cent); research/educational institutes (10 per cent); and commercial and private users (28 per cent).

While the majority of ReliefWeb's users are from North America and northern Europe, by early 1997, ReliefWeb was recording users from over 100 countries. Lack of equipment, expertise, and access in developing countries are important issues which must be addressed. DHA is making efforts to reach those relying on less sophisticated information technology. For example, IRIN-GL makes use of e-mail networks to disseminate its information throughout Africa and the world. Electronic-formatted documents can be downloaded from ReliefWeb and disseminated via e-mail or shared on diskette. In the future, materials may also be available on CD-ROM.

DHA Information Sources

"DHA-Online" provides access on the Internet (http://www.reliefweb.int/dha_ol) to DHA materials on humanitarian affairs, including emergency reports, United Nations Inter-Agency Consolidated Appeals, the donor contributions database, the periodic *Humanitarian Newsletter*, the Landmines Database, an abstract of the Military and Civil Defence Assets manual, and other information derived from the DHA mandate. "DHA-Online" describes the work of the Department in everything from disaster management training to humanitarian diplomacy. It also includes extensive documentation on the International Decade of Natural Disaster Reduction (IDNDR) and DHA efforts in natural disaster mitigation and preparedness.

Next steps

No single agency or system is capable of meeting all the information needs of those preparing for and responding to humanitarian crises and disasters. What is necessary is a sustained commitment to promote and support collaborative efforts in information collection, analysis, exchange and dissemination. While those devising preventive strategies and those launching multilateral responses may have differing needs, all stand to benefit from an increased exchange of information.

The DHA information tools including HEWS, IRINs and ReliefWeb—are the first step towards a strategic information framework which could support humanitarian action by all major actors. In the future, there will be a need for: increased and improved reciprocal communication between field and headquarters; standardized situation reporting from field offices through the use of agreed guidelines; more inter-agency information exchange agreements; and additional field-based networks. DHA plans to continue providing the United Nations system and other humanitarian partners with rapid and widespread access to information, and to a broad choice of information products. In keeping with the volatile nature of emergencies, DHA will remain flexible enough to expand and contract the field-based portions of the information structure as emergencies flare up and subside, while still allowing sufficient monitoring and analytic capacity for early-warning purposes. To effectively coordinate in the field of information, the ERC must manage a rational, targeted, and cost-effective information system supporting all aspects of humanitarian operations■

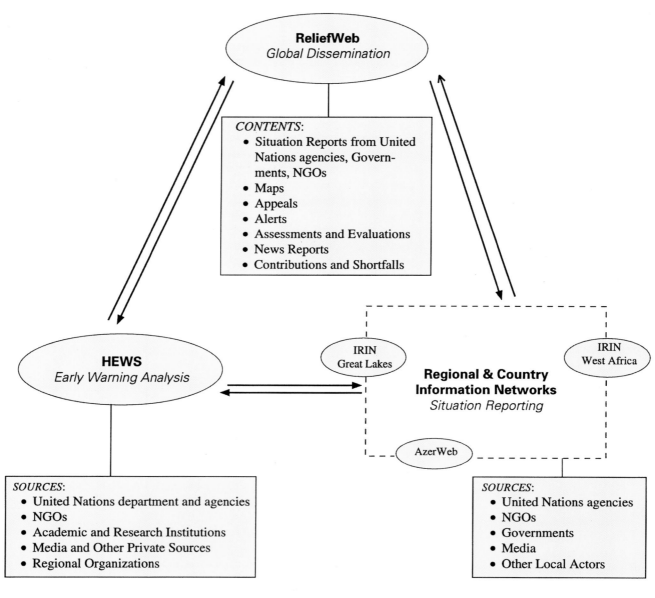

FIGURE 16. *The DHA integrated approach to information.*

Part Two

Major developments in emergency relief coordination, 1996-early 1997: complex emergencies and natural disasters

Chapter 4

The Great Lakes Region of Central Africa

FIGURE 17. *Small child in a long column of women and others returning home after up to two years as refugees in Zaire.* [UNICEF/HQ96-0696/Roger Lemoyne]

In recent years the epicentre of the crisis in the Great Lakes region of Central Africa has shifted quickly from country to country:

- **1993:** political and ethnic conflict and widespread violence in **Burundi**, following the assassination of first elected Hutu President;

- **April-July 1994:** full-scale genocide of 800,000-1,000,000 people in **Rwanda** and the subsequent exodus of 1.7 million Hutu refugees into eastern Zaire, Tanzania and Burundi, including a substantial number of former Hutu military, militia and political leaders;

- **After July 1994:** an unsettled situation in the refugee camps particularly along **Zaire**'s borders with Rwanda and Burundi;

- **1995:** escalation of ethnic violence in **Burundi**; and

- **1996:** another cataclysmic chapter occurred in the tragic history of the Great Lakes region, with its epicentre in **Zaire**.

Background

Warning signals of a looming socio-political crisis in eastern **Zaire** and along its borders with **Rwanda** and **Burundi** had been evident ever since the refugee camps were established in the middle of 1994. In early 1996, ethnic tensions broke into violence in Masisi when elements of the Hutu-led ex-Armed Forces of Rwanda (FAR) and the Interahamwe militia joined local Zairians of Hutu origin to attack the local Zairians of Tutsi origin. In October, unrest spread from Uvira to North Kivu province, this time pitting the Zairian Tutsi population against the Zairian Armed Forces (FAZ), allegedly supported by armed Hutu elements of the Burundian Forces for the Defence of Democracy (FDD), as well as the Rwandan ex-FAR and Interahamwe. In November 1996, the Tutsi rebels joined with the Alliance Démocratique des Forces de Libération du Congo-Zaire (ADFL), a political alliance of four Zairian opposition parties forged by Laurent-Désiré Kabila as an instrument to topple President Mobutu. By April 1997, the rebel alliance had gained control of more than half of Zaire—including the vital river port of Kisangani and the second largest city, Lubumbashi—and was progressing towards the capital Kinshasa, intent on taking control of the entire country.

One of the first steps taken by ADFL was to assume control of the huge refugee camps in Uvira, Bukavu and Goma, along Zaire's borders with Burundi and Rwanda. This resulted in the repatriation of approximately 600,000 refugees back to Rwanda during November 1996, with 150,000 more returning over the following months (see map II overleaf). A similar repatriation movement of 400,000 refugees took place from the camps in Tanzania in December 1996. By January 1997, 1.2 million refugees had returned to Rwanda from Tanzania and Zaire.

This massive return, while a positive development, posed a major challenge for **Rwanda**. Within two months, 15 per cent of its population had to be reintegrated, straining the political and social structures of the country and complicating its economic reconstruction efforts.

In **Burundi**, the ongoing political crisis peaked in July 1996 after a *coup d'état* by Major Pierre Buyoya, the former Tutsi leader who had taken power in 1987 and played a significant role in bringing the country to democratic elections in 1993. Both Hutu opposition groups and extremist elements of the Tutsi minority subsequently intensified their anti-Government activities, first in the countryside and then in the capital, Bujumbura.

Major Buyoya's *coup* was interpreted in the region and by the broader international community as an anti-constitutional act which

POPULATION MOVEMENTS IN THE GREAT LAKES REGION (OCTOBER 1996 - MARCH 1997)

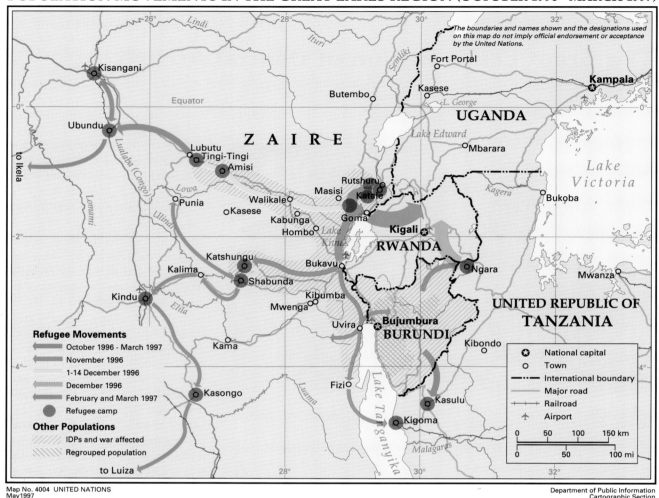

Map No. 4004 UNITED NATIONS
May 1997

Department of Public Information
Cartographic Section

MAP II

could lead to further instability in Burundi. On 31 July 1996, neighbouring countries imposed comprehensive economic sanctions—covering food, medicines, medical supplies, agricultural implements, vehicles, spare parts, industrial equipment, supplies and fuel. No exemptions were made on humanitarian grounds. International flights were also affected, resulting in the virtual isolation of the country. The sanctions were substantially relaxed by the Fourth Arusha Summit on the Conflict in Burundi in April 1997 and food and medicines are now exempted.

All observers agree that these interrelated crises in the Great Lakes are in essence, political and that their implications are regional. Thus any outside political initiatives must be crafted for the entire region. A number of peacemaking efforts have been undertaken since 1993 by the United

Nations in Burundi and Rwanda, and by the Organization of African Unity (OAU), the European Union (EU) and individual countries throughout the region.

After the fighting in eastern Zaire escalated in October 1996, the United Nations sought to address the political aspects of the crisis by appointing Mr. Raymond Chrétien as Special Envoy of the Secretary-General. In November, the Security Council authorized the deployment of a Canadian-led multinational force (MNF) which was intended to facilitate humanitarian assistance, the voluntary repatriation of refugees and the return of internally displaced persons (IDPs) to their homes (resolution 1080 (1996)). The MNF was not fully deployed, however, partly due to the unexpectedly rapid massive return of Rwandan refugees from eastern Zaire. At the turn of the year, an estimated 400,000 Rwandan and Burundian

refugees were believed to have remained in eastern Zaire.

In order to address the escalating fighting in Zaire and the security problems in Burundi, as well as the difficulties experienced by Rwanda in reintegrating the returnees and the risk of further instability spreading throughout the region, the United Nations and OAU Secretaries-General appointed, in January 1997, Ambassador Mohamed Sahnoun as their Joint Special Representative for the Great Lakes region. The Security Council subsequently adopted resolution 1097 (1997), containing a five-point peace plan proposed by Ambassador Sahnoun. The plan stipulated:

- Immediate cessation of hostilities;
- Withdrawal of all external forces, including mercenaries;
- Reaffirmation of respect for the sovereignty and territorial integrity of Zaire and other States of the Great Lakes region;

- Protection and security for all refugees and displaced persons and facilitation of access for humanitarian assistance; and
- Rapid and peaceful settlement of the crisis through dialogue, the electoral process and the convening of an international conference on peace, security and development in the region.

On 27 March 1997, an OAU summit meeting at Lomé adopted a declaration which, in substance, mirrored the United Nations plan.

Humanitarian needs

The volatility of the conflicts in both Zaire and Burundi, the limited access to affected civilian populations and the deteriorating security situation in western Rwanda have made it very difficult to determine the exact locations and numbers of refugees, IDPs and other war-affected persons in the Great Lakes region and to make comprehensive assessments of humanitarian needs.

However, by April 1997, United Nations agencies estimated that at least 2.9 million Rwandan, Burundian and Zairian persons in the Great Lakes region were in need of external humanitarian assistance to avoid imminent malnutrition or death. Approximately 330,000 refugees from Rwanda and Burundi were still in eastern Zaire, and 16,000 Rwandan refugees in Uganda. About 160,000 Zairian refugees were also scattered in the region and an uncertain number of Zairians was internally displaced. Some 280,000 refugees from Burundi were in Tanzania, and there were an estimated 500,000 IDPs and regrouped people in Burundi. In addition there were 1.4 million recent returnees in Rwanda.

In **Zaire,** the major humanitarian challenge has been to gain access to the refugees as well as the growing numbers of internally-displaced and war-affected persons. Access to provide humanitarian assistance is limited for several reasons:

- Security and administrative restrictions in ADFL areas and along the military front;
- Systematic looting by the retreating Zairian army; and
- Severe deterioration of roads, airstrips and other transportation infrastructure, creating major logistical difficulties.

Living conditions dramatically worsened for Rwandan and Burundian refugees who lost their main source of subsistence when they left the camps in October/November 1996, as well as for internally displaced Zairians who were forced to leave their land or urban dwellings. There have been disturbing reports of serious human rights violations.

In **Burundi,** an estimated 500,000 persons are internally displaced or gathered in camps. Additionally, 200,000 Burundians have sought refuge in Tanzania since the 1996 *coup*, adding to the 70,000 Burundian refugees already there. Some 40,000 are estimated to be in Zaire. The escalating fighting and the negative impact of sanctions have resulted in a rapid deterioration in the living conditions of the civilian population. Even the rural population—able to cope more easily than the urban populations at the early stages of the embargo—has begun showing increasing signs of malnutrition as agricultural production has decreased. The Burundian Government's policy of forced regroupment of up to 270,000 mainly Hutu civilians from rural areas into camps poses a major dilemma for humanitarian organizations, which find themselves caught between their vocation to assist people in need and their principled opposition to policies which clearly violate human rights. The United Nations has established clear guidelines for the provision of humanitarian assistance to those in regroupment centres which must: encompass only life-sustaining supplies; require independent ongoing needs assessments and monitoring; and stipulate full and free access by human rights observers. In April, the communiqué of the Fourth Arusha Summit on the Conflict in Burundi and resolution 1997/77 of the Commission on Human Rights each condemned the practice of regroupment and called for it to be dismantled.

In **Rwanda,** in addition to the ongoing needs for humanitarian and reintegration assistance to the 1.4 million recent returnees, longer-term programmes for economic rehabilitation, development and social reconciliation must be mounted if the country's fragile society is to be rebuilt. Repair and construction of shelters, the reorganization of the patrilineal land tenure system so that it can accommodate the needs of the high number of female-headed households, and investment in economic activities that can absorb an excess agricultural labour force are all priority needs. As a necessary precondition for social reconciliation in Rwanda, in parallel with the work of the International Criminal Tribunal on Rwanda, an efficient and fair national criminal justice system must be built in order to hold accountable the leaders and perpetrators of the genocide.

The Rwandan Government is preparing an Emergency Rehabilitation

FIGURE 18. *Returning home after up two years as refugees in Zaire, people on the road between the towns of Gisenyi and Kigali in Rwanda.* [UNICEF/HQ96-0692/Roger Lemoyne]

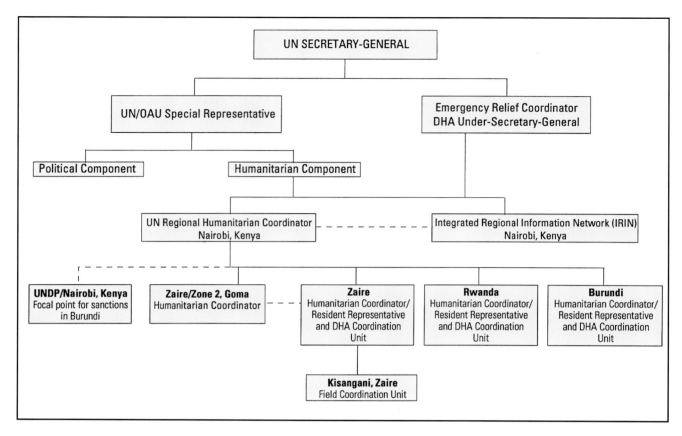

FIGURE 19. *Humanitarian coordination structure for the Great Lakes region, March 1997.*

and Reconstruction Programme for submission to the donor community, but, thus far, international funding for such programmes in Rwanda has lagged far behind the requirements. The deteriorating security situation in the western part of the country further jeopardizes the effective use of available resources.

In addition to these needs in the three affected countries, the pro-longed presence of refugees and internally displaced persons has imposed severe economic and environmental strains on local communities which have provided asylum. In both eastern Zaire and western Tanzania, large areas have been deforested and local economies disrupted by inflation, competition for resources and other distortions. This has resulted in growing local hostil-ity against the refugees, particularly in eastern Zaire. Uganda also faces the prospect of more Rwandan, Burundian and Zairian refugees spilling over its borders, as do Angola, Malawi and Zambia. Unfortunately, the humanitarian needs in the Great Lakes region are likely to fester and spread until such time as peace settlements are reached in both Zaire and Burundi and social stability is achieved in Rwanda.

Humanitarian response

The continuing crisis in the Great Lakes has required one of the largest international humanitarian efforts in the 1990s. (See figures 21 and 22). Until late 1996, DHA humanitarian coordinators in Rwanda, Burundi and Zaire worked at the country level while operational agencies such as UNHCR, UNICEF and WFP worked both on the country level and on a regional basis. In March 1996, donors which had joined together to analyse the 1994 response of the international community to the humanitarian crisis caused by the genocide in Rwanda, recommended, among other things, that regional humanitarian coordination be strengthened in the

FIGURE 20. *Distribution of firewood to Rwandan refugees, in an effort to reduce environmental damage caused by more than one million refugees, Kahindo camp, North Kivu, Zaire.* [UNHCR]

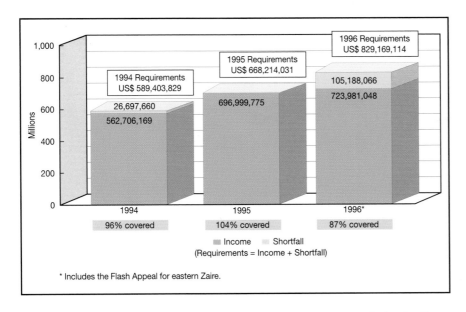

FIGURE 21. *History of United Nations Consolidated Inter-Agency Appeals for the Great Lakes Region (value in US dollars).*

Great Lakes (see box on Lessons from the Rwanda experience, page 43). In November 1996, as the security situation in eastern Zaire rapidly deteriorated and massive outflows began from the refugee camps, on the advice of IASC, the United Nations Secretary-General appointed a Regional Humanitarian Coordinator (RHC) for the Great Lakes. Sergio Vieira de Mello, Assistant High Commissioner for Refugees, initially served in this capacity, followed by Martin Griffiths, Director of DHA, and Pierce Gerety, Regional Representative of UNICEF for the Great Lakes Region. (See figure 19, page 40.)

The RHC has tried to facilitate the work of humanitarian organizations which are facing formidable challenges:

- a violent and rapidly changing situation;
- limited access to populations in need;
- continuing abuses of the human rights of non-combatants;
- threats to the security of humanitarian workers; and
- an inadequate logistics infrastructure.

Assisted by a small office in Nairobi, the RHC has contributed much-needed strategic guidance for the United Nations Humanitarian Coordinators based in Rwanda, Burundi and Zaire; the United Nations Resident Coordinators based

in Tanzania, Uganda and Kenya; and the Regional Representatives from the operational agencies—mainly UNHCR, UNICEF and WFP. The RHC monitors the overall implementation of the regional programme, travelling regularly to negotiate with national and local authorities on access for humanitarian personnel and relief supplies to populations in need.

Given several fatal attacks on humanitarian workers in Burundi and Rwanda, and serious looting in Zaire, the RHC has also brought pressure on national and local authorities to prevent further attacks, and to better ensure the security of relief workers

in accordance with humanitarian law. The RHC has raised the concerns of the humanitarian community with United Nations officials, Governments and regional organizations conducting political negotiations in the region—particularly the Joint Special Representative of the United Nations and OAU, Ambassador Sahnoun, and the country-based Special Representatives of the Secretary-General. The Secretary-General, the High Commissioner for Refugees, and the Emergency Relief Coordinator, Under-Secretary-General Akashi, have frequently pressed for continued access to those in need and for all parties to respect humanitarian principles and law.

At the operational level, DHA works through the existing coordination arrangements of the United Nations agencies. UNHCR coordinates all refugee-related matters, particularly in the border areas of Zaire; WFP coordinates food aid and logistics; and WHO monitors the health status of affected populations.

Many of the mechanisms for emergency coordination available to DHA have been utilized during the Great Lakes crisis:

- The Integrated Regional Information Network for the Great Lakes region (IRIN-GL), established in 1995, collects, analyses and disseminates information on daily events and longer-term develop-

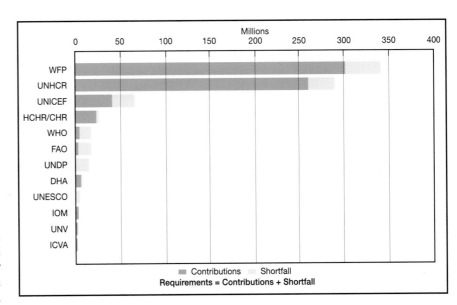

FIGURE 22. *1996 United Nations Consolidated Appeals for the Great Lakes Region (including the Flash Appeals for Eastern Zaire) by appealing organizations (value in US dollars).*

41

FIGURE 23. *Returning home after two years as a refugee in Zaire, a boy carrying a jerrycan, with a bundle on his head, walks along the road between the towns of Gisenyi and Kigali, Rwanda.* [UNICEF/HQ96-0697/Roger Lemoyne]

ments in the region. At the height of the 1996 crisis in eastern Zaire, IRIN produced twice-daily situation reports which were widely used by United Nations agencies, donor Governments, NGOs and the media; currently IRIN is producing a daily update;

- Multinational stand-by teams from Denmark, Sweden and the United Kingdom were deployed

to provide infrastructure for the RHC, the Humanitarian Coordination Unit in Burundi and the Field Coordination Unit in Rwanda;

- The Military and Civil Defence Unit (MCDU), at the request of the operational agencies, was utilized to draw on military resources for humanitarian operations in the region; and

- Two United Nations Disaster Assessment and Coordination (UNDAC) missions were dispatched to Rwanda, eastern Zaire and Tanzania in November and December 1996.

Given the highly volatile situation in the region, in November 1996, the Secretary-General launched the United Nations Inter-Agency Flash Appeal for Eastern Zaire, seeking US$ 259 million to cover the three-month period of November 1996-January 1997. In mid-March, a Consolidated Inter-Agency Appeal for the Great Lakes Emergency in Eastern Zaire, Burundi and Tanzania for 1997 was launched for US$ 325 million. At the request of the Government of Rwanda, that country was not included in the 1997 regional appeal; the United Nations is consulting with the Government to assist it in meeting Rwanda's current needs.

The appeal serves as a platform for all United Nations agencies and NGOs—UNHCR, WFP, UNICEF, WHO, FAO, HCHR/CHR, UNESCO, UNV, ICVA and DHA—to appeal for funding of their emergency programmes in a coordinated manner ■

FIGURE 24. *New school in Matouga, Kibungo Province, Rwanda, April 1996.* [Harald Brandsberg]

"The international response to conflict and genocide: Lessons from the Rwanda experience"[1]

Summary of findings and recommendations

Finding: Humanitarianism cannot substitute for political action.

Recommendation: Need for policy coherence in the Security Council/General Assembly and in the United Nations Secretariat.

Action: The fact that humanitarianism cannot be used as a substitute has now become a mantra, thanks in part to the results of this study. The humanitarian community now has greater access to the Security Council, both through the office of the ERC and through informal consultations with NGOs and others.

Finding: Lack of security in refugee camps.

Recommendation: Need to work with host governments to disarm militants, separate them from genuine refugees, prevent military training in refugee camps, halt operations of hate media, and split large camps into smaller ones farther from an international border.

Action: While a few camps were split into smaller ones, no other actions taken by the international community. In 1996, the ADFL military campaign disbanded the refugee camps.

Finding: Inadequate early warning of population displacements and sudden increases in relief needs.

Recommendation: Establish a field-based integrated humanitarian early warning system.

Action: Strengthened early warning of population displacements through enhanced reporting, but relief hampered by lack of access.

Finding: Mixed performance in coordination.

Recommendation: More unified and effective coordination among and by official agencies, including:
- strategic coordination by Regional Humanitarian Coordinator; and
- operational coordination among individual agencies responsible for specific activities, with common services agreements, as required.

Action: The Regional Humanitarian Coordination Office was established in November 1996 and improvements in operational coordination and common services took place.

Finding: Mixed performance of non-governmental organizations (NGOs).

Recommendation: Professional NGO performance evaluation, including the option of accreditation.

Action: ICVA, an NGO consortium, appointed a regional representative in Nairobi in December 1996. Burundi and Zaire's Field Coordination Units incorporated NGOs.

Finding: Unclear role of military contingents in humanitarian relief operations.

Recommendation: Systematic assessment of cost-effectiveness of military compared with non-military contingents in humanitarian relief operations.

Action: Advance teams for a multinational force (MNF) were withdrawn after 1.2 million refugees returned to Rwanda in November-December 1996. The Secretary-General stated in February 1997 that access to remaining refugees in eastern Zaire would have been facilitated by deployment of MNF.

Finding: Weak accountability.

Recommendation: System-wide monitoring and evaluation mechanisms.

Action: No system-wide monitoring and evaluation, but new coordination and information mechanisms are steps towards better accountability.

Finding: Adverse impacts on local populations and environment.

Recommendation: Minimize adverse local impacts through strengthening local capacities and coping mechanisms.

Action: Except in Rwanda, adverse local impact was not systematically addressed due to access and security obstacles.

Finding: Inequitable food distribution.

Recommendation: More equitable food distribution.

Action: Generally improved, but volatility requires ongoing assessments and adjustments.

---

[1] Steering Committee of the Joint Evaluation of Emergency Assistance to Rwanda, Strandberg Grafisk, Odense, Denmark (1996).

Chapter 5

Afghanistan

Background

After more than 17 years of fighting, displacement and destruction, the protracted conflict in Afghanistan continues to have grave implications for the Afghan population and for stability in the region. Throughout 1996, the Taliban fought forces allied to the Government and other groups, and expanded their control of the southern and western provinces until they captured Jalalabad and Kabul in September. After Kabul fell to the Taliban on 27 September, a new alignment of opposition forces saw the emergence of the Supreme Council for the Defence of Afghanistan (SCDA), composed of the National Islamic Movement of Afghanistan, led by General Rashid Dostum,

the Jamiat-I-Islami, led by Barhanuddin Rabbani and Commander Ahmed Shah Massoud, and the Hezb-I-Wahdat, led by Karim Khalili. With the Taliban having consolidated their position in the southern and central two thirds of the country, fighting continued on two main fronts: in Badghis Province and in the strategically important Ghorband Valley west of Charikar, which leads to the central highlands and the north of the country.

Over the past year, the United Nations has continued to seek a negotiated solution to this ongoing crisis through the United Nations Special Mission for Afghanistan (UNSMA), first under the leadership of Mr. Mahmoud Mestiri and, subsequently, Mr. Norbert Holl. In early 1996, the

Special Mission began consultations with Afghan leaders while Kabul remained under siege by the Taliban, and these discussions continue with both the SCDA and the Taliban leadership. In January 1997, Under-Secretary-General Yasushi Akashi travelled to Afghanistan, meeting with Taliban authorities in Jalalabad and with the Chairman of the SCDA, General Abdul Dostum, in Mazar-I-Sharif. In both meetings USG Akashi stressed that settlement of the conflict was a prerequisite for durable solutions to humanitarian problems. A number of initiatives have been taken by UNSMA to unblock the dialogue among and between the Afghan parties about a cease-fire agreement and durable peace, but so far without success.

FIGURE 25. *Nursing students, Chal de Wardak Hospital, Wardak Province, Afghanistan.* [Karla Schefter]

POPULATION MOVEMENTS IN AFGHANISTAN (OCTOBER 1996 - MARCH 1997)

Map No. 4001   UNITED NATIONS
May 1997

Department of Public Information
Cartographic Section

MAP III

Humanitarian needs

Afghanistan is one of the poorest countries in the world, ranking 170th of the 174 countries in the Human Development Index and having the highest rate of infant, childhood and maternal mortality in Asia.[1] The long war has produced a refugee population which currently stands at least at 2.6 million, of which 1.4 million are in Iran and 1.2 million in Pakistan. In addition, there are from 500,000 to 1,200,000 internally displaced persons within Afghanistan.

Humanitarian conditions, however, vary considerably; some parts of the country are experiencing severe emergency needs, while others enjoy relative stability and economic recovery. The escalating fighting and political developments of the past year have

---

[1] *Human Development Report 1996*, UNDP, New York.

significantly affected the provision of humanitarian assistance to several parts of the country and aggravated existing needs. The upsurge in fighting in the fall of 1996 displaced at least 300,000 people from two areas: Badghis Province and areas around Kabul. Ongoing fighting has driven an estimated 150,000 from Charikar and other villages in the Shomali Valley towards Kabul; some 50,000 people from Badghis, mostly towards Herat; and 100,000 from Kabul and surrounding areas towards the northern provinces and into Pakistan (see map III). These displaced persons increase pressures on the local populations who are already facing difficult living conditions. In addition, concern has been expressed by the United Nations and the international donor community that continued fighting and political instability have limited their ability to implement ongoing programmes.

By contrast, in more stable areas, almost four million Afghans who had fled their country have returned in recent years and are working to rebuild their livelihoods. In certain parts of the country, children have been immunized, mines have been cleared, and widows and the disabled have received loans to start small businesses. Relief organizations continue to provide assistance in many communities. United Nations agencies hope that local authorities will encourage persons displaced from these more stable regions to return home, particularly ethnic Tajiks who were displaced from the Shomali Valley north of Kabul. In the southern provinces of Ghazni, Helmand, Kandahar, Nimruz, Oruzgan and Zabol, the cessation of fighting and the establishment of local authority by the Taliban have restored a measure of security. On the other hand, Taliban policies, especially restrictions on the employment of local female staff in humanitarian projects

45

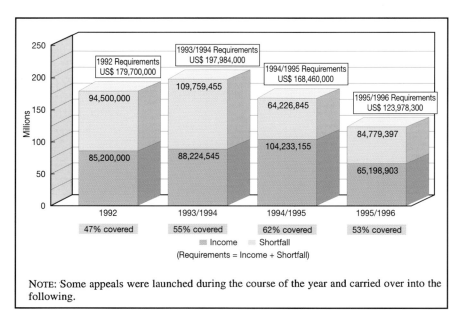

Figure 26. *History of United Nations Consolidated Inter-Agency Appeals for Afghanistan (value in US dollars).*

Humanitarian response

and limits on access to female beneficiaries have created additional complications for the implementation of humanitarian assistance programmes. (See box on Gender issues in Afghanistan, page 48.)

Established just after the Geneva Accords of April 1988, the United Nations Office for Coordination of Humanitarian Assistance to Afghanistan (UNOCHA) was one of the first special arrangements responsible for promoting and coordinating humanitarian assistance in a complex emergency. In 1992, DHA assumed oversight of UNOCHA. UNOCHA has a broad range of responsibilities for coordination, resource mobilization, the management of logistics and telecommunications operations, the humanitarian demining programme, and the provision of emergency information. Because of continued fighting and the resultant insecurity, the UNOCHA main office remains in Islamabad, Pakistan, with sub-offices in Kabul and throughout Afghanistan, as well as in Termez, Uzbekistan, and Peshawar, Pakistan.

Despite the changing military and political landscape in 1996 and reduced funding from the international community, United Nations agencies, ICRC and a large number of NGOs have continued to assist vulnerable Afghan groups. In the cities, particularly Kabul, food aid, shelter materials and medical assistance are provided primarily to female-headed households, widows, the disabled and the elderly. A variety of food-for-work schemes, such as WFP bakery projects in Kabul or a tile-making factory in Herat, continue throughout Afghanistan. In some areas of the country, United Nations agencies and other relief organizations provide emergency assistance to both internally displaced persons and local communities, including food aid, health and sanitation, voluntary repatriation, mine-related activities, and agricultural and rehabilitation assistance. As a priority, United Nations agencies and their humanitarian partners are working to create an environment conducive to the resettlement and reintegration of IDPs. UNICEF, UNHCR, UNOPS and HCHR/CHR are involved in integrated community-based projects, often with support from the WFP food-for-work activities. Vocational training programmes have been developed to facilitate peaceful reintegration and to rebuild local capacities and institutions.

One essential precondition of the successful return of IDPs and refugees to their homes is reducing the estimated 9.7 million anti-personnel landmines still deployed in the country. The demining programme in Afghanistan—one of the oldest and most successful of those coordinated by the United Nations—includes four components: mine clearance; mine awareness; mine clearance training; and a national mine survey. The bulk of the work is undertaken by Afghan NGOs and coordinated by UNOCHA. By December 1996, the demining programme had cleared some 60 square kilometres of battlefield and 100 square kilometres of other terrain. During 1997, it aims to clear 28 km^2 of mined settlement areas, 20 km^2 of former battlefields, survey 20 km^2 of other land, provide mine awareness training to 600,000 people and increase the use of dogs in the clearance of mines. New mines, however, are being laid as the fighting continues.

Prior to the fall of Kabul, the protracted conflict in Afghanistan had become one of the world's "forgotten crises". The support of the donor community for United Nations CAPs for Afghanistan has declined. (See figures 26 and 27.) While the 1994-1995 Appeal attracted 62 per cent of the required funds, the subsequent 1995-1996 appeal received only 53 per cent and a supplement issued in October 1996 for emergency winter needs, particularly in Kabul, received virtually no support.

After the fall of Kabul in September 1996, continued fighting between Taliban and Government forces refocused some attention on Afghanistan. The consequences of this fighting, the targeting of civilians and humanitarian workers, restrictions on access to populations in need, and the effects of the harsh winter—combined with the need to balance longer-term development efforts in some areas of the country with efforts to meet the most pressing emergency needs elsewhere—created major challenges for the humanitarian community.

To determine how to proceed in this environment, DHA and UNDP, supported by the Government of the Netherlands, convened an International Forum of Assistance to Afghanistan in Ashgabat, Turkmenistan from 21-22 January 1997. Chaired by the Emergency Relief Coordinator, Under-Secretary-General Akashi, and attended by some 250 representatives of United Nations agencies, donor Governments, NGOs and a range of Afghan

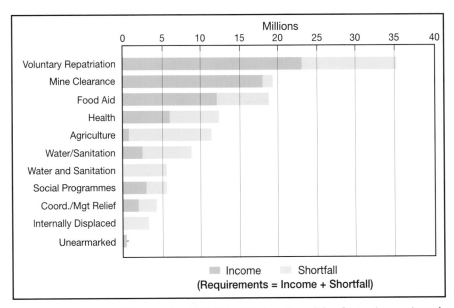

FIGURE 27. *October 1995-December 1996 United Nations Consolidated Inter-Agency Appeal for emergency assistance and rehabilitation for Afghanistan, by sector (value in US dollars).*

participants, the Forum drew on a major ''lessons learned'' study of the nine-year-old humanitarian programme in Afghanistan.[2] The Forum agreed on the need for a common assistance strategy that would combine interrelated elements of emergency assistance, peacemaking, peacebuilding, and development. The strategy would emphasize certain key principles:

[2]*Afghanistan: Coordination in a Fragmented State*, by Antonio Donini, Eric Dudley and Ron Ockwell, DHA, United Nations (December 1996).

- the priority of humanitarian concerns;
- the need to respect human rights;
- the impartiality of aid providers;
- support for the peace process; and
- the participation of the Afghan population, both local authorities and community groups.

To improve United Nations coordination, the Forum also agreed to strengthen the presence of the United Nations system inside Afghanistan and to link more closely the political and the humanitarian/development

components of United Nations work in the country. Following discussions between DHA and UNDP, together with other IASC participants, it was agreed that the Humanitarian Coordinator would also assume concurrently the responsibilities of the United Nations Resident Coordinator.

In December 1996, Under-Secretary-General Yasushi Akashi launched the 1997 Consolidated Appeal for Assistance to Afghanistan, requesting US$ 133 million for 1997. In contrast to the relatively poor response to recent appeals, donor interest in this new appeal has been considerable. Although the Forum was not a pledging conference, several donor Governments indicated support for the 1997 Consolidated Appeal. The Forum's conclusions suggest that the international community is ready to increase further its support to Afghanistan where and when there is peace and stability, as long as international norms and standards are respected. Follow-up discussions between the Humanitarian Coordinator and the warring parties have continued to highlight the key humanitarian principles emphasized at the Forum and to pursue consideration of issues such as gender equality and the repatriation of displaced persons ∎

FIGURE 28. *Food distribution in Kabul, Afghanistan, in January 1997 by ICRC, an international humanitarian organization which is independent of the United Nations system.*

Gender issues in Afghanistan

The economic and social conditions that affect the status of women in Afghanistan fall well below international standards. Afghanistan ranks last on the list of 130 countries in the UNDP Gender-Related Development Index, which tracks issues such as female literacy, income, life expectancy and school enrolment.[1] Afghan women have also been put at risk by the internal conflict which began in 1979.

In November 1995, announcements were made by the Taliban movement restricting the education and employment of women in some parts of Afghanistan under their control. More recently, and particularly since the take-over of Kabul by the Taliban in September 1996, the Taliban have enacted measures severely limiting the human rights of women and, in particular, their access to education and health. Most female local staff of United Nations agencies and NGOs—except for those employed in the health sector—have not been permitted to work. Their exclusion not only makes the implementation of relief and development programmes difficult, but also seriously affects the longer-term development of the society as a whole. For example, the education sector, where the majority of teachers are women, is being substantially weakened.

In October 1996, the Secretary-General called for the respect of the rights of women and girls in Afghanistan and stressed the "single, [UN] system-wide policy on the question of gender equality". In resolution 51/195 of 17 December 1996, the General Assembly denounced "discrimination against girls and women and other violations of human rights and international humanitarian law" and noted "with deep concern possible repercussions on international relief and reconstruction programmes in Afghanistan".

This situation and the "conditionality of aid" have been the subject of much debate. UNICEF has declared that no education programme will be supported unless access is given to both male and female students. Little progress has been made in ensuring access of women to education and employment. While exceptions to the Taliban restrictions have been reported in some areas, when Afghan schools opened in March 1997, very few girls were permitted to enter. By contrast, in Kabul and other Taliban-controlled areas, WFP has been able to implement bakery and carpet-weaving projects expressly for widows which, as food-for-work projects, have allowed women to continue to be involved in the planning and implementation of assistance programmes.

Agencies are struggling to find ways to continue their work while meeting the needs of all members of Afghan society. The International Forum for Assistance to Afghanistan stressed that further "programme options" must be developed which are acceptable both to the Afghan authorities and to donors. To help develop a strong system-wide policy on this issue, a DHA team recently concluded a visit to Afghanistan and its findings will help IASC and the United Nations agree on a unified and clear position for the international community.

---

[1] *Human Development Report 1995*, UNDP, New York.

Chapter 6

The Sudan

FIGURE 29. *Porters prepare to load sacks of food into the hold of a United Nations/Operation Lifeline Sudan airplane at Lokichokio airport in Kenya. The food will be air-dropped into isolated regions of southern Sudan.* [UNICEF/C-113/Betty Press]

Background

Civil war between the Government of the Sudan and southern Sudanese opposition movements has continued unabated for fourteen years. Fighting intensified between Government forces and the principal opposition movement, the Sudanese People's Liberation Movement/Army (SPLM/A), throughout 1996. In mid-1996, groups opposed to the Government of Uganda also increased attacks on Sudanese refugee and humanitarian workers in camps in northern Uganda and on humanitarian convoys serving internally displaced persons (IDPs) in areas of southern Sudan close to the Ugandan border. A series of major military offensives in late 1996 and early 1997 on several fronts in eastern and southern Sudan generated flows of more than 100,000 newly displaced persons in these areas.

On the political front, peace initiatives undertaken since 1993 by the Intergovernmental Authority on Development (IGAD) came to a standstill in 1995 because of deteriorating diplomatic relations between Eritrea, Ethiopia and Uganda, on the one hand, and the Government of the Sudan, on the other. In January 1996, the Security Council adopted resolution 1044 (1996) upon the complaint of the Government of Ethiopia relating to the Sudanese Government's alleged involvement in the June 1995 assassination attempt against President Hosni Mubarak of Egypt. Further political developments, following Security Council resolutions asking the Sudan to comply with its requests for the extradition of the suspects involved in the assassination attempt and a cessation of alleged Sudanese Government support for international terrorist groups, have dimmed prospects for resuming dialogue among IGAD member States. (See box on sanctions overleaf.)

Humanitarian needs

More than a million persons are estimated to have died in Sudan's civil war, and as many as four million Sudanese have been displaced or have sought refuge abroad. In 1996, war-affected persons throughout the country, already living below subsistence levels, struggled to cope with the effects of chronic malnutrition and an alarming increase in the spread of infectious diseases such as AIDS, kala-azar, cholera and severe diarrhoeal diseases. The Government's own efforts to provide humanitarian assistance were compromised by the rapid deterioration of the economy in 1996 and the resulting loss of foreign exchange and purchasing power on the local market.

FIGURE 30. *Eleven-year-old John Kathara (far left), reunited with his family, Leer, southern Sudan.* [UNICEF/OLS/Radhi Chalasani]

Assessing the humanitarian impact of sanctions on the Sudan

In January 1996, the Security Council requested the extradition from the Sudan of three suspects believed to have fled to that country following the June 1995 assassination attempt on the life of President Hosni Mubarak of Egypt in Addis Ababa, Ethiopia (resolution 1044 (1996)).

In April 1996, the Security Council reiterated this request and imposed sanctions against the Sudan: reducing the number of Sudanese diplomatic personnel and restricting the entry and transit of Sudanese Government officials on missions abroad (resolution 1054 (1996)).

In August 1996, given the continued non-compliance of the Sudan with the requests contained in the two earlier resolutions, the Security Council adopted resolution 1070 (1996) which stated:

"... that all States shall deny aircraft permission to take off from, land in, or overfly their territories if the aircraft is registered in Sudan, or owned, leased or operated by or on behalf of Sudan Airways or by any undertaking, wherever located or organized, which is substantially owned or controlled by Sudan Airways, or owned, leased or operated by the Government or public authorities of Sudan, or by an undertaking, wherever located or organized, which is substantially owned or controlled by the Government or public authorities of Sudan."

The Council also decided that it would set a date for this flight ban to take effect and determine the means of implementing it after 90 days, so that the Government of the Sudan could comply with previous resolutions. The Security Council also asked the Secretariat to provide information on the potential humanitarian impact of the flight ban on the Sudanese population before it would actually be imposed.

In December 1996, DHA prepared a report on the possible humanitarian impact of the flight ban on the provision of basic food and health care services, based on preliminary assessments undertaken by United Nations agencies in Khartoum. The Department was then asked to provide additional information on the potential humanitarian impact of the flight ban. Accordingly, DHA dispatched an expert to the area for three weeks in January-February 1997, to elaborate on the preliminary assessments with regard to the health sector, the supply of food and other essential services to the Sudanese population, and the conduct of relief operations in the Sudan.

The expert travelled to Lokichokio, Kenya, where he visited the OLS logistics base for the Southern Sector, and to Khartoum, where he held meetings with Government officials in several ministries; United Nations agencies, including UNICEF, WFP and WHO; the International Committee of the Red Cross; and representatives of international and local non-governmental organizations.

In February 1997, Under-Secretary-General Yasushi Akashi presented to the Security Council the expert's report, which covered:

- the cost of evacuating critically-ill patients to hospitals outside the Sudan;
- the possible effect of the flight ban on imports of life-saving drugs;
- the impact of the flight ban on domestic air transport as it might affect the supply of basic food and health care services; and
- the potential impact of the flight ban on relief operations.

The main findings of the report were:

- The imposition of the flight ban envisaged in Security Council resolution 1070 would impair the capacity of the public health authorities to facilitate specialized medical treatment for critically-ill patients outside the country.
- Given the dependence of domestic air carriers on offshore maintenance, a flight ban could have a serious impact on national immunization programmes, domestic distribution of drugs and food production.
- Emergency food assistance in Government-controlled areas in the south did not substantially rely on domestic air transport. Most of the food assistance there was provided by OLS and was delivered either by air from Kenya, using aircraft registered outside the Sudan, or by road and river. The supply of food assistance thus should not be affected by the flight ban. However, the logistics of the food assistance providers such as WFP could be affected by the flight ban since they used domestic air carriers for transporting equipment and personnel; and
- The flight ban might hinder the operational capacity of large providers of non-food assistance, such as UNICEF and international NGOs, by interrupting their operations until they raised the funds to operate independently from domestic air carriers.

Since the presentation of the expert's report, no final determination has been made by the Security Council on the implementation of resolution 1070 (1996).

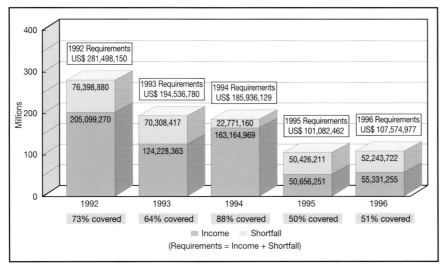

FIGURE 31. *History of United Nations Consolidated Inter-Agency Appeals for the Sudan (value in US dollars).*

International humanitarian relief efforts were also severely hampered by intensified fighting and the unwillingness of the warring parties to provide reliable access to persons in need. The Government of the Sudan imposed several restrictions on Operation Lifeline Sudan which included:

- a total flight ban on all humanitarian aircraft;
- a no-fly zone for areas along the Ugandan border;
- a denial of flight clearances to locations severely affected by the spread of cholera and severe diarrhoeal diseases; and
- interdiction of the use of a C-130 large cargo aircraft.

In mid-1996, following the refusal of the Government of the Sudan to provide clearance for humanitarian flights into rebel-held areas of the southern Sudan, over 1,800 persons died from cholera and diarrhoeal diseases, and deliveries of WFP food commodities from Lokichokio, in northern Kenya, were reduced by 80 per cent.

In retaliation against the Government's refusal to grant access for relief activities in rebel-held areas, rebel factions also began denying access to certain Government-controlled areas of southern and central Sudan. This further constrained the ability of humanitarian agencies to meet the needs of vulnerable populations.

In addition to reduced access, threats against humanitarian workers also increased in 1996. More than 60

evacuations were undertaken, involving approximately 240 relief personnel in 35 separate locations in southern Sudan: up 50 per cent from the number of evacuated staff in 1995. Relief workers also reported five hostage-takings and 37 separate bombing incidents in areas inhabited by civilian populations.

The intensified hostilities blocked attempts by Mr. Vieri Traxler, the Secretary-General's Special Envoy for Humanitarian Affairs for the Sudan, to restart negotiations with the parties on improving humanitarian access. A realignment among rebel movements took place after one major group signed a Political Charter with the Government in April 1996; this further complicated

the task of identifying legitimate interlocutors for a resumption of these talks. Fresh efforts to resume negotiations will be made when Mr. Robert van Schaik, who was appointed in April 1997 to succeed Mr. Traxler, visits the region.

Humanitarian response

The United Nations established Operation Lifeline Sudan (OLS) in April 1989 to avert mass starvation of civilians displaced or otherwise affected by the armed conflict in southern Sudan. Since that time, OLS has evolved from a short-term relief operation to a wide-ranging emergency humanitarian relief effort. OLS works with all parties to the conflict in Government-controlled and rebel-controlled areas to facilitate the delivery of humanitarian assistance both within and from outside the country. OLS was one of the first United Nations mechanisms for humanitarian coordination that sought to assist IDPs and war-affected civilians in an ongoing conflict within a sovereign country, as opposed to assisting refugees beyond its borders. As such, OLS has been an important model for humanitarian coordination missions in other countries impacted by civil conflict.

Overall authority for OLS activities within the Sudan is vested in the United Nations Coordinator for Emergency and Relief Operations (UNCERO), based in Khartoum. He

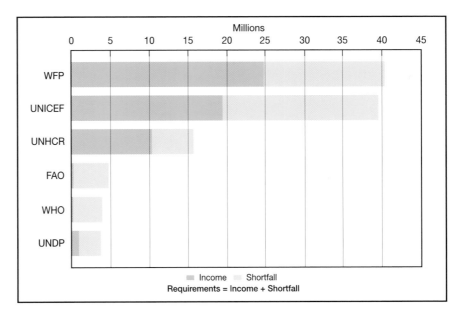

FIGURE 32. *1996 United Nations Consolidated Inter-Agency Appeal for the Sudan, by appealing organizations (value in US dollars).*

FIGURE 33. *Unaccompanied minors prepare meals, Natinga, southern Sudan.* [UNICEF/OLS/Radi Chalasani]

is supported by a field coordination unit, which also functions as the focal point for coordinating humanitarian activities carried out in the OLS Northern Sector by the six United Nations humanitarian organizations which participate in the annual United Nations CAP for the Sudan—FAO, UNDP, UNHCR, UNICEF, WFP and WHO—and over fifty international NGOs based in Khartoum. (See map IV, page 53.)

In 1989, when rebel control extended over most of southern Sudan, the parties to the conflict agreed to the establishment of an OLS Southern Sector coordination office in Nairobi and an OLS operational base in Lokichokio, northern Kenya. OLS activities in the Southern Sector cover both Government and rebel-held areas in southern Sudan and are supervised by an OLS coordinator based in Nairobi, who functions under the overall authority of UNCERO. Whereas the working relationship between United Nations agencies and NGOs based in Khartoum remains somewhat ad hoc, in

the Southern Sector over 30 international NGOs have signed letters of understanding with the OLS Nairobi office, creating a veritable consortium of United Nations and NGO relief programmes on behalf of OLS.

Since the fighting intensified in late 1995 in southern Sudan, lack of security, denial of access to vulnerable areas and logistical difficulties have all seriously limited the delivery of humanitarian relief. In 1996 OLS delivered 50,000 tonnes of food relief. Of this amount, 29,000 tonnes were allocated to Government-controlled areas throughout the country and 22,000 tonnes to areas controlled by the rebel movements. OLS also delivered by air more than 3,000 tonnes of non-food supplies to areas accessible from Lokichokio, Kenya, and continued to support programmes in the fields of health, household food security, livestock, water and sanitation, emergency education, war-affected children and capacity-building. While in absolute terms, these delivery figures were close to the goals set at the outset of the year, Government restrictions on OLS activities in the south resulted in considerable delays in reaching affected populations, particularly from April to September, the season of most acute food shortages.

Since 1992, successive CAPs for the Sudan have raised US$ 597 million. In 1995 and 1996, funding declined considerably; between 1992 and 1994, United Nations agencies raised an average of 75 per cent of their funding requirements, while in 1995 and 1996, international donors covered no more than 51 per cent of the already reduced requirements. (See figures 31 and 32.) As of early April 1997, the current appeal has raised only about 5 per cent of its required funding.

Given continuing problems of humanitarian access, lack of security and limited funding, in late 1995, the IASC agreed to commission a team of international experts to undertake the first comprehensive review of OLS. (See box on OLS Review,

page 54.) In September 1996, DHA convened separate meetings to discuss the final conclusions of the OLS Review with representatives of the Government of the Sudan, the three southern movements which participate in OLS, donor governments and international relief organizations.

Based on the Review's findings, the humanitarian agencies will work to improve the delivery of assistance in the Sudan by negotiating with the parties to obtain the following:

- Protection and security of international relief personnel and convoys;
- Clearance of OLS flights from Lokichokio, Kenya, to affected areas of southern Sudan;
- Extension of the two 1994 agreements on OLS humanitarian access, facilitated by the then Intergovernmental Authority on Development and Drought, to include relief deliveries across confrontation lines and related monitoring procedures;
- Agreement by the Government of the Sudan on improved operational procedures for international NGOs based in Khartoum;
- Humanitarian access to certain areas of critical need, including rebel-held areas of the Nuba Mountains; and
- Strict adherence of the parties to OLS guidelines and principles, particularly the neutrality and independence of United Nations humanitarian relief agencies and OLS-associated international relief organizations in carrying out assessments, monitoring and evaluation, relief aid allocation and distribution.

It remains to be seen if OLS will be able to fully achieve its goals, given the increasing restrictions on humanitarian deliveries in recent years and the concomitant decline in donor support. Unless OLS can increase its effectiveness, the severe curtailment of humanitarian activities which occurred in the Sudan in 1996 could well continue■

UN/OLS EMERGENCY PROGRAMMES IN THE SUDAN

The boundaries and names shown and the designations used on this map do not imply official endorsement or acceptance by the United Nations.

▨	OLS Northern Sector as of December 1996
▨	OLS Southern Sector as of December 1996 including: 1) Government-controlled areas serviced out of Khartoum or out of Kenya by OLS; 2) Rebel-controlled areas serviced out of Kenya by OLS
▢	Drought-affected areas outside OLS served by UN and other international relief agencies
▨	Areas not covered by UN emergency humanitarian or drought-related programmes contained in the 1997 UN Consolidated Inter-Agency Appeal for the Sudan

✪	National capital	—·—·—	International boundary
◉	Regional capital	—·—·—	Regional boundary
○	Town	——	Major road
✈	Airport	········	Railroad

0   100   200   300 km
0   100   200 mi

Map No. 4003   UNITED NATIONS
May 1997

Department of Public Information
Cartographic Section

MAP IV

Plan of action implementing the OLS Review

In September 1996, OLS partners and participating United Nations agencies endorsed a number of the OLS Review's recommendations and agreed on the following strategy for humanitarian programmes in the Sudan:

Humanitarian principles: Together with UNICEF's Child Rights Programme, the United Nations Humanitarian Coordination Unit (UNHCU) will train the Government of the Sudan and other OLS partners in the application of humanitarian principles for civilian populations affected by the ongoing conflict.

Humanitarian access: The Special Envoy for Humanitarian Affairs will negotiate with the parties to the conflict to try to broaden access and formalize operational arrangements. The Special Envoy will seek commitments from all OLS partners to operational standards and humanitarian principles.

Partnership: United Nations agencies will train agencies of the Government of the Sudan in rapid response management, establish capacity-building projects to enhance the economic productivity of civilian populations in rebel-controlled areas of southern Sudan, and develop common contractual agreements with NGOs for increased programme coordination. The United Nations will continue to negotiate collective humanitarian access, offer technical and material assistance to NGOs in both sectors, and provide security training and services to NGOs in the Southern Sector. The United Nations will organize periodic reviews and planning sessions with donors and NGOs to develop a common approach to assessments, access and resource mobilization.

Coordination: In early 1997, headquarters support for the United Nations Humanitarian Coordination Unit in Khartoum was transferred from UNDP to DHA. This change is designed to strengthen the office of the United Nations Coordinator for Emergency and Relief Operations (UNCERO) as the focal point for information-gathering and reporting on OLS activities.

Relief assistance: United Nations agencies will standardize programme assessment methodologies within both OLS sectors, so as to better identify and prioritize appropriate programme needs.

Internally displaced persons: In order to achieve better results in implementing OLS resettlement and rehabilitation strategies, UNCERO will assume a stronger role in coordinating assistance to IDPs. By placing IDP advisers in areas with significant numbers of displaced persons, UNCERO intends to ensure the rights of IDPs to receive humanitarian assistance.

Chapter 7

Iraq: the humanitarian programme and the implementation of Security Council resolution 986 (1995)

FIGURE 34. *In central and southern Iraq, commodities that comprise the food basket under Security Council resolution 986 are given by the Government to private food agents, who then distribute items to families and individuals. May 1997.*

Background

The Gulf War in 1991 and the ensuing widespread civil insurrection caused severe disruption to Iraq's economy and infrastructure, in particular to facilities for power generation and distribution, communications, transport, potable water supplies and sewage disposal. The three northern governorates suffered particularly marked population dislocations in the wake of armed confrontation with Iraqi Government forces.

Following the cease-fire, the Security Council adopted resolution 687 (1991) on 3 April. Since then, the United Nations Security Council has maintained a range of sanctions against Iraq to ensure full compliance with its resolutions relating to the destruction of Iraq's weapons of mass destruction, the recognition of Kuwait's international borders and

the return of Kuwaiti prisoners of war and property. These sanctions have significantly constrained Iraq's ability to earn foreign currency. They have also limited its legitimate imports to humanitarian goods authorized by the 661 Committee: the Security Council Committee established by resolution 661 (1990) which had initially imposed sanctions on Iraq after its invasion of Kuwait.

Humanitarian needs

Although Iraq was able to repair parts of its damaged infrastructure after the cease-fire in 1991, this was insufficient to ensure the civilian population's access to guaranteed safe drinking water and electricity supplies. Moreover, the civilian population was adversely affected by growing unemployment, increased inflation, particularly in food prices, and the widespread destruction of livestock. Notwithstanding the operation of a Government-subsidized food ration in central and southern

Iraq, the income, purchasing power and nutritional status of the civilian population came under sustained pressure. Iraq's public health infrastructure, which had been relatively well developed by regional standards, suffered marked deterioration involving both shortages of medical equipment and supplies and the loss of qualified personnel to more lucrative employment abroad.

Although these problems had become increasingly serious after 1991, a marked deterioration in the nutritional and health status of the population was evident after 1994. A variety of Iraqi, NGO and United Nations reports pointed to increased evidence of malnutrition and associated problems among those most at risk, notably children under the age of five, and an increase in the incidence of low birth-weights. The Government food ration was successively reduced so that by the end of 1996 it provided about 1,275 calories daily: approximately two thirds of WHO and other widely accepted minimum standards of daily caloric

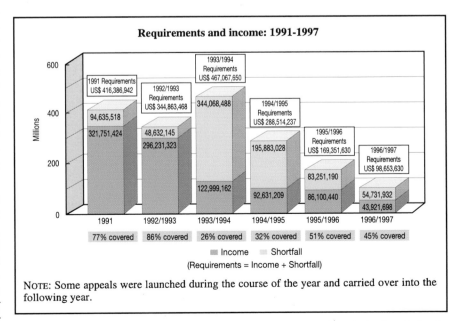

NOTE: Some appeals were launched during the course of the year and carried over into the following year.

FIGURE 35. *History of United Nations Consolidated Inter-Agency Appeals for Iraq (value in US dollars).*

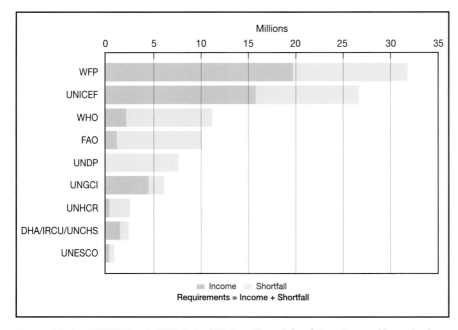

Millions

FIGURE 36. *April 1996-March 1997 United Nations Consolidated Inter-Agency Humanitarian Programme in Iraq, by appealing organizations (value in US dollars).*

86 per cent of the stated requirements. (See figures 35 and 36.) In 1996-1997, 88 per cent of the funds for the humanitarian programme in Iraq has been provided by five major donors: the Netherlands, the United States of America, Sweden, Germany and Japan (see figure 37).

The Humanitarian Programme has encompassed a wider range of projects in the three northern governorates of Dohuk, Erbil and Suleimaniyah than in the rest of Iraq. In the north, the Programme has focused both on the provision of relief assistance to internally displaced persons and refugees and on a range of resettlement initiatives, including a wide variety of infrastructure, health, agricultural and education programmes.

intake. Many United Nations agencies and NGOs observed that the public health care system was also becoming less able to provide sustained or effective treatment, with very serious reductions in the range of treatments available, surgery and emergency services.

Humanitarian response

The United Nations Humanitarian Programme since 1991

In response to the evident needs stemming from the Gulf War and associated disturbances, the United Nations established an Inter-Agency Humanitarian Programme in 1991 to address the requirements of the whole country. This Programme has been coordinated since 1992 by DHA, through the United Nations Office of the Humanitarian Coordinator in Iraq (UNOCHI).

Within the overall programme, specific activities are carried out by FAO, UNDP, UNESCO, UNHCR, UNICEF, WFP and WHO. Successive United Nations CAPs have been launched since 1991 to cover the immediate needs of vulnerable groups for food, agricultural assistance and nutrition, water supply and sanitation services, basic health services, shelter and education. Since May 1991, these appeals have raised a total of US$ 964 million, with a rate of response ranging from 26 per cent to

Humanitarian assistance in response to the 1996-1997 United Nations Consolidated Inter-Agency Humanitarian Programme in Iraq[a]
1 April 1996-31 March 1997

	Donors	Value in US dollars	Percentage of funding
1.	Netherlands	13,845,083	31.51
2.	USA	11,525,000	26.23
3.	Sweden	7,388,820	16.82
4.	Germany	4,632,825	10.54
5.	Japan	1,460,000	3.32
6.	Australia	595,238	1.35
7.	Finland	434,782	0.99
8.	Norway	411,097	0.94
9.	Switzerland	380,228	0.87
10.	France	350,081	0.80
	Others[b]	2,914,760[c]	6.63
	TOTAL	**43,937,914**	**100.00**

Humanitarian assistance in response to 1996-1997 United Nations Consolidated Appeals

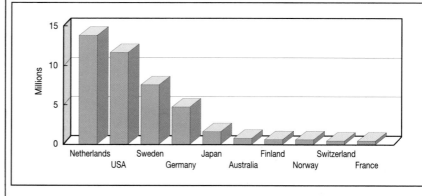

[a] Includes contributions received for emergency requirements for the period October-December 1996.
[b] Others include Cyprus, EC-ECHO, United Nations agencies, Escrow Account and Carryover Funds.
[c] Carryover funds amount to approximately US$ 1.4 million.

FIGURE 37. *Major donors of humanitarian assistance to Iraq in 1996-1996 (value in US dollars).*

It has also provided winter heating fuel as a result of the internal embargo imposed on the region by the Government of Iraq.

In order to ensure the safety of United Nations personnel and assist international NGOs operating in the north, in 1991, the United Nations established the United Nations Guards Contingent in Iraq (UNGCI) to escort convoys and relief workers as well as to provide security assessments. Since its inception, UNGCI has relied on voluntary contributions to fulfil its responsibilities. Currently UNGCI deploys up to 150 personnel, provided by the Governments of Bangladesh, the Czech Republic, Denmark, Greece, Nepal, the Netherlands, the Philippines and Poland.

The implementation of Security Council resolution 986 (1995)

Since 1991, the Security Council has attempted to alleviate the impact of United Nations sanctions on Iraq's civilian population and to meet essential humanitarian needs by a variety of measures which would have allowed Iraq to sell a limited quantity of oil, under United Nations supervision, in order to fund the import of humanitarian goods. The most extensive of these measures was Security Council resolution 986 (1995), which authorized the sale of US$ 2 billion over a period of 180 days to meet the essential humanitarian needs of Iraq's civilian population, as well as other defined purposes such as compensating the victims of Iraq's invasion of Kuwait in 1990.

In May 1996, the Government of Iraq concluded a Memorandum of Understanding (MOU) with the United Nations on the implementation of the resolution. On the basis of the stipulations of SCR 986 (1995), of the US$ 2 billion worth of oil to be sold:

- US$ 1.32 million are to be expended for the procurement of humanitarian supplies, of which:
  - US$ 1,060 million are for the 15 governorates in central and southern Iraq; and
  - US$ 260 million are for the three northern governorates.
- US$ 44 million are to be expended for operational and admin-

istrative expenses of the programme.
- The remaining US$ 635 million are to be disbursed as follows:
  - US$ 600 million to the United Nations Compensation Fund for the victims of Iraq's unlawful invasion and occupation of Kuwait;
  - US$ 15 million to meet the operating costs of the United Nations Special Commission; and
  - US$ 20 million to the escrow account established by Security Council resolutions 706 (1991) and 778 (1992).

As required under the MOU, the Government of Iraq drew up a Distribution Plan for the equitable distribution of goods authorized under the resolution. It included the needs of the three northern governorates that were identified by the authorities in the north, in consultation with the United Nations Humanitarian Programme. This Plan was approved by the United Nations Secretary-General in July 1996. Implementation was delayed as negotiations on outstanding issues took place and the security situation in the north deteriorated, after intervention by Iraqi Government forces in inter-Kurdish fighting. Finally, on 9 December, the Secretary-General informed the Security Council that all actions necessary to ensure effective implementation of SCR 986 (1995) had been undertaken and the Secretariat was ready to proceed. The 180-day period commenced on 10 December 1996.

Implementation of Humanitarian Programme in Central and Southern Iraq

Under the terms of the resolution and MOU, the Government of Iraq is responsible for distributing SCR 986 supplies in the fifteen governorates of central and southern Iraq according to procedures outlined in the Distribution Plan. The overall responsibility for the observation process rests with DHA.

In order to observe the efficiency, equitability and adequacy of the distribution, 151 United Nations international observers are based in Baghdad and travel periodically

throughout the country. They operate in three separate but complementary tiers:

- 75 sectoral observers from several United Nations agencies are responsible, at the national level, for monitoring the distribution of SCR 986 commodities and assessing their effectiveness and equitability in regard to their respective sectors.
- 76 observers have been deployed by DHA in two units.
  - The geographical observation unit in the Office of the Humanitarian Coordinator (UNOHCI) is responsible for observing delivery, storage and distribution at the governorate and district levels and collating relevant data.
  - The multi-disciplinary observation unit in UNOHCI consists of international experts in the areas of food logistics, public health, pharmaceuticals, hospital equipment, water and sanitation, agricultural inputs and machinery, animal health, plant protection, education and electricity. Its principal functions are to increase the range of expertise available in the observation mechanism, to maintain a tracking system for all SCR 986 supplies and to report directly to DHA in New York.

Final analyses of the reporting from the observers based in Iraq will be undertaken by DHA in New York, for consideration by the Secretary-General and the Security Council.

Even though the implementation period under the resolution commenced on 10 December 1996, necessary commercial arrangements delayed the arrival of humanitarian supplies pursuant to SCR 986 (1995). The first proceeds from oil sales did not arrive into the SCR 986 Iraq account until 15 January 1997, and the first letters of credit for the purchase of humanitarian goods were not issued until 14 February. As a result, the distribution of supplies envisaged in the Distribution Plan could not commence before March.

While awaiting the first deliveries, a range of preparatory activities was undertaken by United Nations agencies so as to observe the distribution of SCR 986 supplies. For

HUMANITARIAN PROGRAMME IN IRAQ (SC Res. 986)

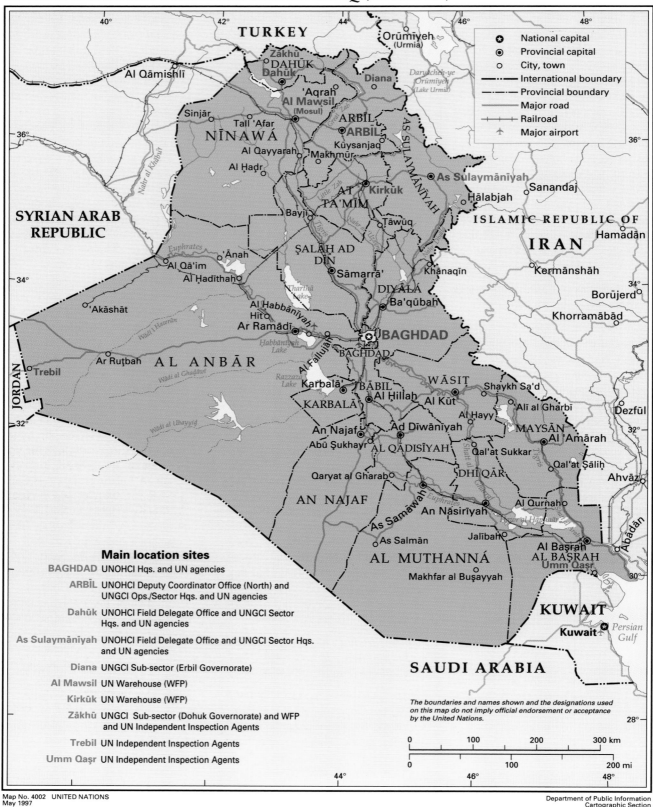

Legend:
- ⊛ National capital
- ◉ Provincial capital
- ○ City, town
- —··— International boundary
- —·— Provincial boundary
- —— Major road
- +—+ Railroad
- ✈ Major airport

Main location sites

BAGHDAD	UNOHCI Hqs. and UN agencies
ARBĪL	UNOHCI Deputy Coordinator Office (North) and UNGCI Ops./Sector Hqs. and UN agencies
Dahūk	UNOHCI Field Delegate Office and UNGCI Sector Hqs. and UN agencies
As Sulaymānīyah	UNOHCI Field Delegate Office and UNGCI Sector Hqs. and UN agencies
Diana	UNGCI Sub-sector (Erbil Governorate)
Al Mawsil	UN Warehouse (WFP)
Kirkūk	UN Warehouse (WFP)
Zākhū	UNGCI Sub-sector (Dohuk Governorate) and WFP and UN Independent Inspection Agents
Trebil	UN Independent Inspection Agents
Umm Qaşr	UN Independent Inspection Agents

The boundaries and names shown and the designations used on this map do not imply official endorsement or acceptance by the United Nations.

0   100   200   300 km
0   100   200 mi

Map No. 4002 UNITED NATIONS
May 1997

Department of Public Information
Cartographic Section

MAP V

example, WHO has trained personnel in government medical warehouses in the operation of a computerized receipt-and-dispatch system. FAO has inspected all warehouses to be used for the storage of plant protection inputs, agricultural equipment and veterinary supplies. UNICEF is adapting an existing computerized tracking system to follow the distribution and utilization of supplies for all designated water and sewage-treatment plants.

The first shipment of SCR 986 goods reached Iraq on 20 March. The Government of Iraq decided to wait until it had a month's supply of any commodity before commencing distribution, partly in order to simplify the tracking of the commodities. In central and southern Iraq, therefore, the first distribution of wheat flour occurred in the April 1997 ration, while in the three northern governorates, the first flour distribution commenced on 14 April, under WFP supervision.

By late April, deliveries of foodstuffs and soap/detergents to Iraq totalled over 300,000 tonnes. Of the three permitted entry points, 88 per cent of deliveries had been delivered to Umm Qasr, 7 per cent through Jordan and 5 per cent through Turkey. (See map V opposite.) As of late April, DHA observers had undertaken some 457 observation missions at mills, storage facilities and ration agents throughout the country. As the sectoral agency responsible for observing food distribution, WFP had also undertaken extensive observation of these facilities using local and international staff.

Implementation of Humanitarian Programme in the three northern governorates

Under the terms of SCR 986 (1995) and the MOU, the Inter-Agency Humanitarian Programme is responsible for the distribution of supplies in the three northern governorates of Dohuk, Erbil and Suleimaniyah. In conjunction with local authorities, WFP has completed a population survey and identified some 8,500 ration agents. The Government of Iraq has assigned warehouses in Kirkuk and Mosul to WFP for the storage of foodstuffs for the three northern governorates. As envisaged in the MOU, it has been determined that the procurement of food and medical supplies for these governorates may be undertaken in the most efficient and cost-effective way through bulk purchases by the Government of Iraq. Since 14 April, WFP has distributed wheat flour purchased under this arrangement to all three northern governorates.

In addition to these food and medical supplies, a wide range of other programmes in the north will be funded under SCR 986 (1995). For example, Habitat is to undertake a shelter and resettlement programme. UNDP/Department for Development Support and Management Services has prioritized the needs of the electricity sector and is overseeing repair projects. DHA is coordinating a mines clearance and awareness programme. UNICEF has undertaken a risk-mapping exercise to identify priority areas for water and sanitation. Although observation is not mandatory in the northern governorates, United Nations personnel will monitor and report on the progress of those programmes in the northern governorates which are funded under SCR 986 (1995).

The future implementation of SCR 986 (1995).

The 180-day implementation period for oil sales under SCR 986 (1995) is due to end on 9 June 1997. At the end of the period, the Secretary-General is due to report to the Security Council on the implementation of the resolution, with particular reference to the efficiency, equitability and adequacy of humanitarian supplies distributed under the resolution. The Security Council and the Government of Iraq are expected to come to an agreement on the possible extension of the arrangements envisaged in SCR 986 (1995) ∎

Chapter 8

Demobilization in Angola and Liberia

In civil conflicts, societies tend to become pervasively militarized. Civilians are deliberately targeted and terrorized to achieve military goals; whole regions or populations are taken over by armed groups whose main motivations are political control and/or financial self-interest; and people of all ages, including the very young, are recruited as fighters.

Much more than a cease-fire is needed to bring sustained peace to societies caught up in civil strife. If functioning political institutions are to be restored, widespread militarization must be reversed. The first stage of such demilitarization is disarmament, followed by demobilization: inducing armed fighters to give up their weapons and to adopt a civilian way of life.

All wars end with some sort of demobilization, however partial. But, in a society torn by internal conflict, ex-combatants must learn to live at peace in the same society with those they have so recently targeted. Although it might seem that allocating substantial resources to demobilizing combatants would be prejudicial to other needy groups, the fates of these larger populations are, over time, closely tied to the success of the demobilization effort. Indeed, many internally displaced persons and refugees have identified demobilization of combatants as a key factor encouraging them to return to their home communities.

Demobilization can only begin once violence has ceased and a peace agreement has been reached. For this, all parties to the conflict must be committed to pursuing their goals through political rather than military means. Equally important, individual fighters must be willing to give up arms as a means of survival and personal gain. If not, they may well resort to banditry or enlist in other armed gangs, even if their leaders are committed to peace. Outside organizations can promote the first of these goals through political mediation and moral persuasion, and the second, through training, education and material assistance to demobilizing soldiers.

A full demobilization generally entails four related phases:

- Disarmament of combatants;
- Quartering and registration of combatants, and meeting their immediate needs as well as those of their families;
- Resettlement of combatants into communities, including the provision of transport and start-up household items, farming tools, etc.; and
- Social and economic integration of combatants and their families into civilian life.

While the international community has recognized the importance of effective demobilization for sustaining peace, implementing such demobilization is a daunting task, for several reasons:

- Necessary conditions for demobilization—training programmes and jobs to occupy those abandoning military service—are rarely present in countries emerging from civil conflict;
- Many participants in civil wars, having spent years of their lives as fighters, are ill-equipped to deal with even the rudiments of civilian life, such as reading, writing, social interactions and the use of currency; and
- Established procedures and institutional arrangements for carrying out demobilization do not yet exist, forcing those responsible for demobilization to create ad hoc mechanisms.

Given the widely recognized need for demilitarization to begin after civil conflicts are brought to an end and the absence of a United Nations or other international organization with the designated responsibility to assist in this area, in certain recent post-conflict situations, DHA has had to take the lead in managing the demobilization process. Its role has been most evident in Angola, since 1995, and in Liberia, since 1996. As of 31 March 1997, demobilization activities are still under way in both countries. The completion of the demobilization and reintegration process will no doubt take several more years. Moreover, the results achieved to date remain uncertain, given the persistence of political tensions and the fragile evolution of political institutions in both countries.

Even at this early stage, however, the differing conditions of demobilization in Angola and Liberia are suggestive:

- Angola is a large country, in which control was contested by two main protagonists. Demobilization was planned over a long period and has encountered numerous delays in execution.
- Liberia is a small country where political power was divided among many shifting armed factions. Its demobilization process was hastily organized and undertaken within a few months.

Hence, these two countries offer two distinct perspectives on the essential process of redirecting a society away from armed strife towards peaceful pursuits.

Angola

Since it gained independence in November 1975, Angola has experienced unremitting civil strife between the Government and the opposition movement, the National Union for the Total Independence of Angola (UNITA). The lengthy civil war—exacerbated by outside intervention, both direct and indirect—was interrupted briefly by the Bicesse Accord of 1991, but resumed in November 1992 when UNITA rejected that month's election results. While there were many reasons for the failure of the Bicesse Accord, incomplete demobilization, as evidenced by the ease with which UNITA rearmed and remobilized its forces, was one major factor.

FIGURE 38. *Woman cooking dinner at Vila Nova Demobilization Camp, near Huambo, Angola, where her husband, a former UNITA soldier, has been demobilized.* [UNICEF/DOI 0123/ Giacomo Pirozzi]

The resumed fighting soon escalated to full-scale civil war, spreading hunger and disease among millions of Angolans. Recognizing the need for an effective large-scale relief operation, and following a decision of the IASC, DHA established the Humanitarian Assistance Coordination Unit (UCAH) in early 1993 to coordinate the work of humanitarian agencies in Angola. With the signing of the Lusaka Protocol in November 1994, these agencies began to shift their attention from life-saving relief activities to the resettlement of refugees and internally displaced persons, demobilization and the pervasive anti-personnel land-mine problem.

Angola was the first instance of intensive involvement by DHA in a demobilization process. The Department assumed a central coordinating role because it recognized demobilization as essentially a civilian task. A Demobilization and Reintegration Office was set up within UCAH to organize the contributions of the humanitarian community to this important component of the peace-building process. At the same time, the United Nations peace-keeping operation—the Angola Verification Mission (UNAVEM III)—played key roles: constructing and maintaining the quartering areas for UNITA troops; collecting and registering their weapons; and maintaining a stable security environment in the vicinity of the quartering areas.

While the Lusaka Protocol recognized demobilization as a key to peace, it provided no details about how the process should proceed. It did, however, establish certain basic parameters:

• The estimated 76,000 UNITA troops should be disarmed and encamped at "quartering areas";

• Some of these troops would then be incorporated in the national army (FAA), and others demobilized;

• Some of the original FAA troops, numbering about 100,000, should also be demobilized; and

• The final size of the national army should be limited to 90,000.

Given the high level of mistrust between the parties, it proved difficult to agree on the location of the quartering areas and to persuade UNITA to begin disarming its fighters (see map VI overleaf). Moreover,

FIGURE 40. *Former UNITA soldier with family at Vila Nova Demobilization Camp, near Huambo, Angola.* [UNICEF/DOI 96/0127/Giacomo Pirozzi]

the construction of the 15 quartering areas—some in very remote parts of the country—was an extremely challenging task. It was only in November 1995 that the first quartering area was opened, with the rest opening during the ensuing months.

Since the beginning of the quartering process, UCAH has been responsible for designing and managing a comprehensive programme of humanitarian assistance that includes:

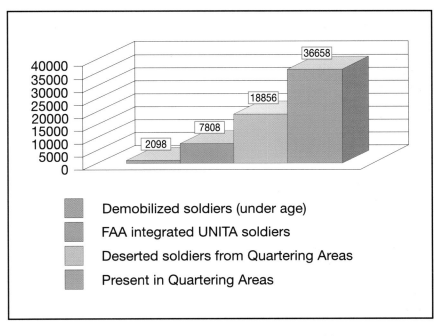

Demobilized soldiers (under age)

FAA integrated UNITA soldiers

Deserted soldiers from Quartering Areas

Present in Quartering Areas

FIGURE 39. *Angola: quartering and demobilization, as of 31 March 1997.*

- identification and registration of UNITA troops;
- collection of socio-economic data to support their reintegration into civilian life;
- distribution of food and non-food items;
- the provision of health, water and sanitation services;
- shelter; and
- civic training projects.

This multi-sector programme has been implemented in association with 11 international NGOs which have professional staff working in the quartering areas, and with the assistance of UNICEF, WFP, WHO and the International Organization for Migration (IOM).

To prepare for the return of former combatants and to help them find a stable livelihood in areas of resettlement, the Government

SELECTION AND DEMOBILIZATION CENTRES IN ANGOLA AS OF 1 APRIL 1997

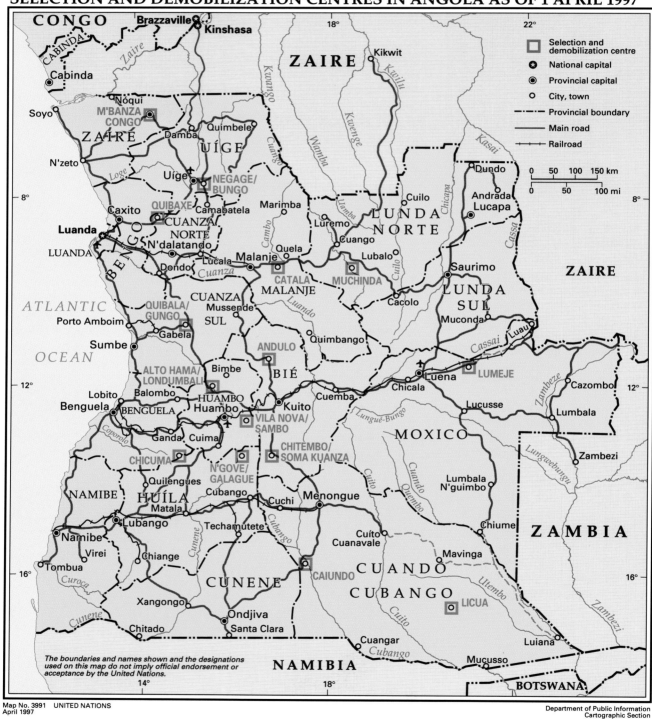

Map No. 3991   UNITED NATIONS
April 1997

Department of Public Information
Cartographic Section

MAP VI

reintegration agency, UNDP and UCAH have designed special training and employment projects, as well as counselling and referral services. UCAH's development of a comprehensive database on the socio-economic profiles of the demobilized soldiers has been particularly useful in the reintegration process.

Owing to continuing distrust between the Angolan Government and UNITA, the quartering phase has lasted much longer than the three-to-five months originally anticipated, and the subsequent steps are proceeding extremely slowly. As of 31 March 1997, only 2,100 under-aged UNITA soldiers had been demobilized; 7,800 UNITA soldiers were incorporated in FAA and 18,600 were selected for the FAA, while 18,900 had deserted the quartering areas (see figure 39). The consequences of the high desertion rate cannot be gauged, as the activities of the deserters are not known.

The protracted process has created a serious security risk and delayed withdrawal of UNAVEM III: placing severe financial strains on donor governments and humanitarian agencies. While demobilization is still in an early stage and large parts of the country remain outside the control of the Government, the formation of the new Government of Unity and National Reconciliation on 11 April is a sign of political progress which could translate into progress in demobilization.

Liberia

Since the outbreak of the civil war in December 1989, Liberia has been at the mercy of half a dozen armed factions. It is estimated that of the pre-war population of approximately 2.3 million, 150,000 have been killed, 768,000 have taken refuge outside Liberia and 750,000 are internally displaced. Lasting peace in Liberia cannot be achieved unless the various factions are disbanded and their fighters demobilized.

Soon after the signing of the Abuja Peace Agreement of August 1995, the IASC requested DHA to establish the Humanitarian Assistance Coordination Office (HACO) in Liberia. Given DHA's experience in Angola, it was decided to assign

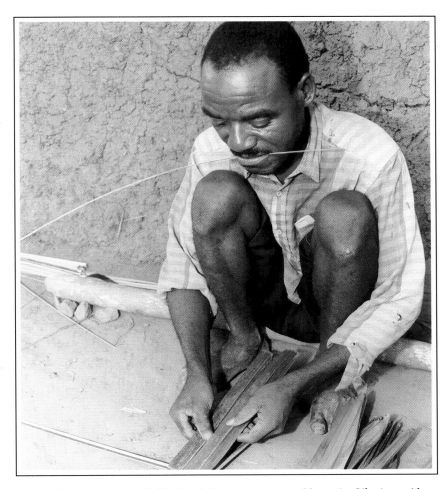

FIGURE 41. *At this Internally Displaced Persons camp near Monrovia, Liberia, residents have set up their own feeding centre and some small cottage industries with help from local and international NGOs. Workers at the camp produce roofing material as part of a programme supported by the Liberian Red Cross and UNDHA-HACO.* [UNDHA-HACO/J. Fecci]

HACO responsibility for demobilization and initial reintegration. A Demobilization and Reintegration Unit was established within HACO to organize the demobilization of combatants and to coordinate programmes to facilitate their return to civilian life.

By March 1996 a disarmament, demobilization and reintegration plan had been completed. It was to be endorsed by the Liberian National

FIGURE 42. *Tubmanburg, Liberia. In September 1996, relief workers reached thousands of civilians trapped by the fighting between two wings of ULIMO. The civilian population was severely malnourished and in need of emergency food and medical aid.* [UNDHA-HACO/K. Page]

Transitional Government when heavy fighting broke out the next month in Monrovia. Virtually all pre-positioned humanitarian stocks were looted during the subsequent factional fighting in April and May, including those set aside for the demobilization programme, and most of the demobilization staff dispersed.

After the signing of the Abuja II Agreement in August 1996, HACO established a Demobilization and Reintegration Task Force, to ensure a coordinated approach by all concerned. The Task Force includes representatives of the United Nations Observer Mission in Liberia (UNOMIL), the Monitoring Group of the Economic Community of West African States (ECOMOG)—the subregional peace-keeping force in

FIGURE 43. *Harper, Liberia. An impromptu demobilization site was created on the last day of disarmament to reach fighters isolated in this remote oceanside town. An ECOMOG soldier verifies that this fighter's weapon is serviceable.* [UNDHA-HACO/K. David]

DISARMAMENT AND DEMOBILIZATION SITES IN LIBERIA (NOVEMBER 1996-FEBRUARY 1997)

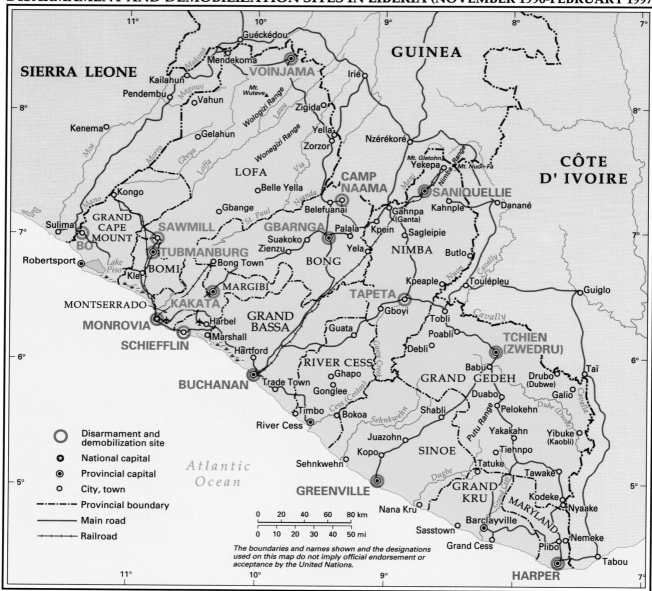

Map No. 3990   UNITED NATIONS
April 1997

MAP VII

Department of Public Information
Cartographic Section

FIGURE 44. *On the final day of disarmament, 31 January 1997, individual fighters from all factions continued to demobilize at this central Monrovia site. A child brings this weapon to ECOMOG, hoping to receive the demobilization package.* [UNDHA-HACO/J. Fecci]

Liberia, United Nations agencies, donors, Liberian Government authorities, and international and local NGOs. The new schedule of implementation of the peace process provided for disarmament and demobilization to begin in November 1996 and to end on 31 January 1997.

Despite the brief notice and an extreme shortage of personnel, logistical and financial resources, HACO began demobilization as scheduled, diverting all of its international humanitarian staff to the effort during the first few weeks. Demobilizing the fighters entailed:

- receiving, registering and interviewing the fighters;
- issuing identification cards;
- providing food and immediate medical assistance; and
- transporting ex-combatants to their areas of resettlement.

A total of 15 demobilization sites were used during the demobilization process, each staffed by one international and some 30 national HACO staff. (See map VII.) WFP, UNICEF and WHO provided crucial support and expertise in their respective fields of competence. The number and location of sites changed as the needs of the programme shifted. At the January deadline, ECOMOG announced a short grace period and the process officially ended on 9 February 1997.

As of 31 March 1997, HACO had demobilized 21,315 of an estimated total of 33,000 combatants, including 4,306 child fighters, many of them suffering the effects of narcotic drugs and traumatized by having been forced to commit violent acts. In addition to those demobilized by HACO, ECOMOG reports having disarmed an additional 4,000-5,000 fighters at checkpoints throughout the country, although these fighters were not officially demobilized (see figure 45).

Besides managing the operational aspects of demobilization, HACO

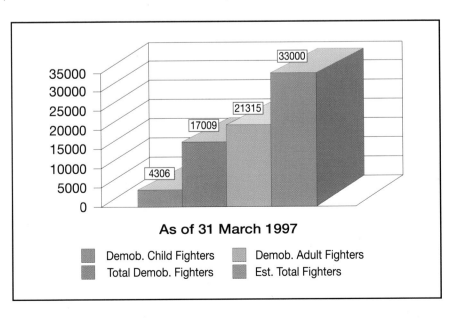

As of 31 March 1997

Demob. Child Fighters   Demob. Adult Fighters
Total Demob. Fighters   Est. Total Fighters

FIGURE 45. *Liberia: disarmament and demobilization.*

65

FIGURE 46. *Fighters from all factions came to this site in Monrovia, Liberia, because for many Monrovia was considered "neutral". This group of fighters came as a unit to disarm. An ECOMOG soldier verifies the serviceability of each weapon.* [UNDHA-HACO/J. Fecci]

The demobilization process—which led to the formal disbanding of the factions at the end of February—has improved the security situation throughout Liberia. It is one factor which has contributed to establishing satisfactory conditions for the scheduled elections which are the next phase of the peace process.

*

* *

It is still too early to draw definitive conclusions from the demobilization efforts in Angola and Liberia, particularly because the crucial reintegration phase has not been started in earnest in either country. This phase will test two design principles that have been incorporated in the current programmes. The first is the importance of developing detailed profiles of the soldiers' socio-economic backgrounds and expectations as a basis for reintegration programmes. The second principle is to integrate assistance for demobilized soldiers with other community development programmes, so as to promote the quickest possible reintegration of former soldiers into civilian life ■

has also taken the lead in coordinating initial reintegration of the combatants. These bridging activities, which are implemented by local and international NGOs and United Nations agencies, include civil reconstruction, vocational training and basic schooling. They focus on both combatants and civilians, in order to ensure the earliest possible reintegration of ex-combatants into civilian life in their communities. A Funding Panel and an Advisory Board, both chaired by HACO and including United Nations agencies, NGOs and donors, have been established to provide policy guidance, review projects and oversee the day-to-day operation and management of projects.

FIGURE 47. *Clara Town, Liberia. Former combatants have created their own self-help group. They have joined a local Civil Reconstruction Team that is helping to dig drainage ditches in their community.* [UNDHA-HACO/J. Fecci]

Chapter 9

Major natural, technological and environmental disasters

In 1992, DHA inherited the United Nations' long-standing involvement in natural disaster assistance from its predecessor organization, the Office of the United Nations Disaster Relief Coordinator (UNDRO), established in 1972. Since 1994, through an arrangement with the United Nations Environment Programme (UNEP), DHA also responds to those environmental emergencies and industrial accidents where international assistance is not otherwise provided under existing specialized conventions or programmes.[1]

Over the past five years, the number of natural, technological and environmental disasters to which DHA has responded has ranged from 54 to

---

[1] See also Part One: chapter 1 on the DHA role in coordinating the international response to natural, technological and environmental disasters; chapter 2 on mobilizing resources for such disasters; and Part Three, chapter 10 on reducing the damage resulting from such disasters.

82 per year—or an average of 68—reflecting cyclical and other fluctuations in weather and in the severity of disasters (see figures 48 and 49.) In 1996, DHA responded to 60 natural and two technological disasters in 46 different countries. In addition, in the first three months of 1997, DHA responded to 13 natural disasters in 12 countries. Map I on pages 4 and 5 shows where and in what manner DHA responded. A quick and effective international response to sudden-onset disasters of all types—natural, technological and environmental—remains an important priority for DHA.

Disaster response mechanisms

DHA helps mobilize and coordinate assistance from the international community to disaster victims by distributing information, channelling immediate cash assistance, dispatching in-kind support, and providing technical assistance.

- *Situation Reports.* DHA issues situation reports on the impact and needs arising from serious natural, technological and environmental disasters and distributes them to donor Governments, United Nations agencies, other international organizations, and non-governmental organizations.

  o In 1996, DHA issued 180 situation reports on major disasters in 46 countries. They were distributed to 400 organizations;

  o In the first three months of 1997, DHA issued 38 situation reports on major disasters in 14 countries.

- *Mobilization of Cash Contributions.* After a disaster, DHA issues international appeals for

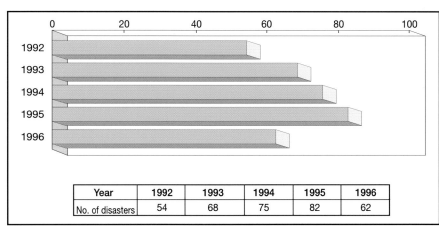

Year	1992	1993	1994	1995	1996
No. of disasters	54	68	75	82	62

FIGURE 48. *Number of natural, technological and environmental disasters in which DHA became involved, 1992-1996.*

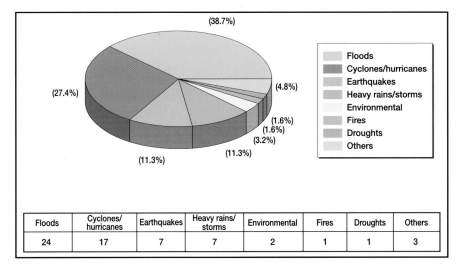

Floods	Cyclones/hurricanes	Earthquakes	Heavy rains/storms	Environmental	Fires	Droughts	Others
24	17	7	7	2	1	1	3

FIGURE 49. *Types of disasters to which DHA responded in 1996.*

funds on behalf of countries seeking international assistance.[2]

- In 1996, DHA issued 27 international disaster appeals. The international community provided US$ 84 million in cash and in-kind contributions, of which US$ 6.2 million was channelled through DHA, with the rest provided directly by donors to the country concerned. In 1996 DHA also directly provided emergency cash grants of US$ 680,000 to seven countries (see figure 11, page 28).

- In 1997, through 31 March, DHA has issued eight new international appeals and has disbursed US$ 240,000 for disasters in seven countries.

- **Shipments of relief items.** Utilizing materials stockpiled at DHA's Pisa Warehouse, DHA provides resources not locally available for relief efforts.

  - In 1996, DHA responded to natural disasters in five countries with six in-kind shipments.

  - In the first three months of 1997, the Pisa Warehouse made five shipments to three countries in response to natural disasters.

- **UNDAC Teams.** United Nations Disaster Assessment and Coordi-

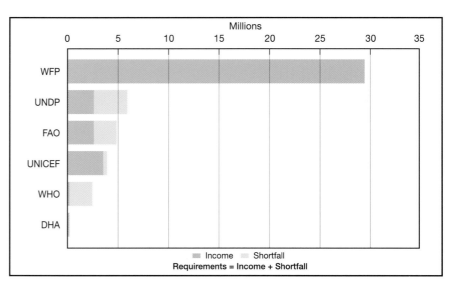

FIGURE 51. *July 1996-March 1997 United Nations Consolidated Inter-Agency Appeal for Flood-Related Emergency Humanitarian Assistance to the Democratic People's Republic of Korea, by appealing organizations (value in US dollars).*

nation (UNDAC) Teams—consisting of DHA Relief Coordination Officers and emergency response managers seconded by Governments—provide rapid needs assessments, assist with telecommunications and information management, and help establish on-site coordination mechanisms.

  - In 1996, UNDAC Teams conducted seven missions in response to natural disasters.

  - In the first three months of 1997, DHA deployed one UNDAC Team in response to floods in Malawi.

- **Environmental assistance.** Under the aegis of the Joint UNEP/

DHA Environment Unit, DHA is bringing international assistance to countries facing such environmental emergencies as industrial accidents, chemical and oil spills and forest fires.

  - In 1996, the Joint Unit responded to requests for assistance from the Philippines, the Russian Federation, Rwanda and Slovenia.

  - In the first three months of 1997, the Joint Unit has provided assistance to Armenia, Chile, Georgia, Moldova, Somalia and Tanzania.

DHA response to major disasters in 1996

1. Democratic People's Republic of Korea (DPRK): floods

Disaster . . . Unusually heavy floods in July-August 1995 triggered severe food shortages throughout the DPRK and caused extensive damage to the agricultural sector—resulting in the destruction of crops and stored grain, soil erosion and the loss of large areas of arable land. The floods swept away entire villages, knocked out large bridges and dams, and destroyed irrigation systems, schools, health clinics and rural hospitals. The DPRK Government estimated the long-term damage at approximately US$ 15 billion.

Almost exactly one year later, once again widespread flooding in July-August 1996 dealt another severe blow to the country's agricul-

---

[2] In complex emergencies, DHA issues Consolidated Inter-Agency Appeals on behalf of United Nations agencies.

FIGURE 50: *People make their way across a river bed after the regular bridge was washed away by flooding in Unpa County, DPRK.* [WFP/Tom Haskell]

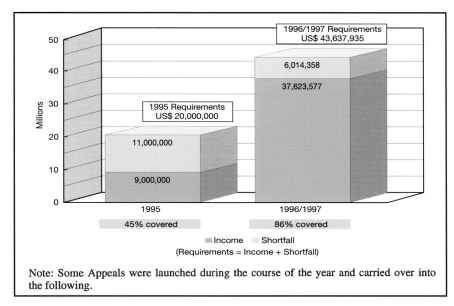

FIGURE 52. *History of United Nations appeals for the Democratic People's Republic of Korea: requirements and income from 1995-1996 (value in US dollars).*

ture. Although these floods were not as heavy as those of 1995, they were concentrated in the southwest of the country, which produces 60 per cent of the country's grain harvest, mainly rice. The Government estimated this latest damage at approximately US$ 2.2 billion.

The cumulative effects of the floods compounded various economic and structural problems, not only harming flood-affected areas, but also extending to virtually the entire population. A joint FAO/WFP Crop and Food Assessment Mission in November 1996 found that the food situation had deteriorated dramatically in the previous year, resulting in an estimated current grain shortfall of 2.36 million tonnes.

Humanitarian response ... At the request of the DPRK Government, DHA launched an international appeal in September 1995 which sought US$ 20 million for food and non-food items. As the economic situation deteriorated in the flood-affected areas, in June 1996 DHA launched a Consolidated Inter-Agency Appeal for Flood-Related Emergency Humanitarian Assistance to the DPRK, on behalf of WFP, UNDP, UNICEF, FAO and WHO, requesting US$ 44 million for the period July 1996-March 1997. In response to the new devastation caused by the 1996 flooding, DHA reiterated the need to support fully the ongoing United Nations Consolidated Inter-Agency Appeal. Donor re-

sponse to the 1995 and 1996 Appeals for the DPRK raised approximately 45 per cent of the amount requested in 1995 and some 86 per cent of the amount requested in 1996-1997 (see figures 51 and 52).

On 7 April 1997, DHA launched another CAP for the DPRK, calling for US$ 126 million for the period April 1997-March 1998. The Appeal listed the most urgent humanitarian needs as food aid, food security projects to further the resumption of normal food production, and the restoration of basic health services, particularly children's nutrition and

health. As of mid-April, approximately US$ 34 million or 27 per cent of requirements had been raised, virtually all towards the food requirements of WFP.

2. China: snowstorms, earthquake and floods

Disaster ... From the end of 1995 to early 1996, many counties in mountainous areas of Sichuan and Qinghai provinces were hit by record low temperatures and unusually heavy snowstorms, affecting 200,000 people. In February 1996, a strong earthquake in Yunnan Province affected 1.2 million people, leaving 322 people dead and 17,000 injured. In the summer of 1996, flooding in 12 provinces affected 200 million persons and left close to 3,000 dead, 243,000 injured and 4.4 million homeless. The economic loss due to the flooding was estimated at US$ 20.5 billion.

Humanitarian response ... Although China has a well-developed disaster management capacity, the Government indicated that it would welcome international assistance to support the relief operations following these three widespread disasters. In response, DHA issued 14 situation reports about their scope and the resulting emergency needs. More than US$ 33 million were reported to DHA in cash and in-kind contributions to assist in these disasters, of

FIGURE 53. *"Alternative" foods comprise the major portion of this meal being eaten by an elderly couple in a typical household in Hungnam, South Hamgyong, DPRK. Dishes are made from wild herbs, maize, pine tree bark and seaweed purchased at the local market. The couple recently resorted to bartering personal items, including a sofa, clothes and a sewing machine to augment family income, 90 per cent of which is spent on food to supplement government rations. The last Government food ration received was reportedly in mid-March and was only 1 kilogram for the entire family.* [WFP/Tun Myatt]

which US$ 1.7 million were channelled through DHA.

3. Central America: hurricane

Disaster . . . Between 28 and 31 July 1996, Hurricane Cesar cut a swath across Nicaragua and Costa Rica, causing extensive flooding and damage:

- In Nicaragua, the hurricane affected about 100,000 people in several regions of the country, or 1.8 per cent of the population. Damage was most severe in areas along the Atlantic coast. The hurricane destroyed thousands of houses and severely damaged some 30,000 hectares of agricultural land, as well as food crops.

- In Costa Rica, the hurricane affected up to half a million people, 17 per cent of the total population. At least 30 people died and housing, roads, bridges and aqueducts were all severely damaged.

Humanitarian response . . . At the request of the Government of Nicaragua, DHA launched an appeal for international assistance. DHA also issued six situation reports and deployed an UNDAC Team to assist with assessments and field coordination of the relief response. US$ 4.2 million in total assistance was reported to DHA, of which US$ 352,709 was channelled through the Department. Together with the DHA emergency grant of US$ 30,000, these funds were used to make local purchases of food supplies, construction materials and medicines.

At the request of the Government of Costa Rica, DHA launched an appeal for international assistance. US$ 4.3 million in assistance was reported to DHA, with US$ 310,000 channelled through DHA to finance relief assistance. In addition, DHA's emergency grant of US$ 30,000 was used to purchase locally available construction materials.

4. Yemen: floods

Disaster . . . In June 1996 heavy rains and floods struck several regions of Yemen, causing extensive damage to villages and towns. Authorities confirmed that 324 people died, 108 persons were missing, 20,000 people were homeless and another 10,000 were affected. Infrastructure—including roads, irrigation canals, water pumps, community power stations and water embankments—was severely damaged and a large amount of agricultural soil was washed away. Economic losses were estimated at US$ 1.2 billion.

Humanitarian response . . . Following a Government request for international assistance, DHA sent an UNDAC Team to help the Government and the DHA Resident Coordinator conduct rapid needs assessments and to establish an on-site operations coordination centre. DHA also issued nine situation reports and dispatched two experts for the rehabilitation of roads, bridges and power installations. Cash and in-kind contributions by the United Nations system, bilateral donors and NGOs to-

FIGURE 55. *Honduras: caught in the floods.* [DHA/Carlos Pereira]

talled over US$ 10 million, of which US$ 834,000 was channelled through DHA. After the emergency phase, DHA and UNDP assisted the Yemeni Government in formulating a national framework for rehabilitation and reconstruction.

5. The Philippines: environmental disaster

Disaster . . . In March 1996, there was a major spill of wastes from the tailings pit at a large copper mine on Marinduque Island. This disaster destroyed the primary food-producing areas of several hundred people and significantly degraded the local environment. Two major rivers were so contaminated that they were considered to be biologically dead.

Humanitarian response . . . In April-May 1996, at the request of the Government, the Joint UNEP/DHA Environment Unit sent an expert mission to the accident site to help national authorities assess the consequences of the spill. After examining existing data and samples of the affected areas and meeting with relevant authorities, the team recommended ways to address the damage and avoid future disasters. These recommendations were shared with national authorities, UNDP, other United Nations agencies, international organizations and concerned private companies ■

FIGURE 54. *Damage to residential area in Yemen, June 1996.*

Part Three

Continuing challenges for humanitarian coordination

Chapter 10

The reduction of natural, technological and environmental disasters

FIGURE 56. *Typhoon-damaged house, Bangladesh.* [UNICEF]

Costs and causes

In 1996, natural disasters, such as storms, floods, landslides and earthquakes, killed 14,000 persons and caused US$ 7.9 billion in direct damage. Total economic losses from natural disasters in 1996 are estimated at some US$ 50 billion, roughly the annual average for the past 25 years. Exceptional disasters can, of course, cause far more damage: in 1995, the earthquake in Kobe, Japan caused 6,000 deaths and damage amounting to US$ 109 billion.[1]

Experience has shown that disaster damage is usually under-reported. Published estimates in the immediate aftermath of disasters—and even at later stages—focus primarily on direct physical damage, rather than on the far greater indirect costs of production and income losses, forced unemployment, and increased costs of basic services induced by disasters. Even direct effects which appear relatively small can, on occasion, have far-reaching and disproportionate consequences. For example, the destruction of a single bridge may lead to the ruin of an entire region's economy for a prolonged period. At the national level, disasters in such countries as Guatemala and the Philippines create average, annual losses of up to 3-4 per cent of the country's gross national product (GNP). With losses of this magnitude, it may take a developing country over 20 years to repay loans contracted after natural disasters: a major constraint on its sustainable development.

Naturally occurring phenomena—whether geophysical, oceanographic, atmospheric or a combination of them—would elicit little public concern if human settlements were not affected. Such natural phenomena constitute a disaster precisely because they adversely affect those human societies located in their path. Population growth, the imperatives of material survival, trade, competition and economic interdependence have rendered it inevitable that growing numbers of people are living in areas at risk. For this reason, the impact of natural disasters has also continued to increase.

In order to mitigate and reduce the harmful effects of natural, technological and environmental disasters, it is necessary to:

---

[1] See Swiss Reinsurance Company, *Sigma*, Nos. 3/1997 and 2/1996; see also Reuters news item, 25 July 1995, quoting an official report of the Japanese Economic Planning Agency.

FIGURE 57. *This 1988 flood disaster in Bangladesh, an aftermath of the heavy monsoon rains, affected up to 30 million of the country's total population of 110 million and left an estimated 28 million homeless. An inflated inner tube is improvised as a shopping basket in waist-high waters. The boys also carry goats on their shoulders.* [UNICEF/Masud Ali]

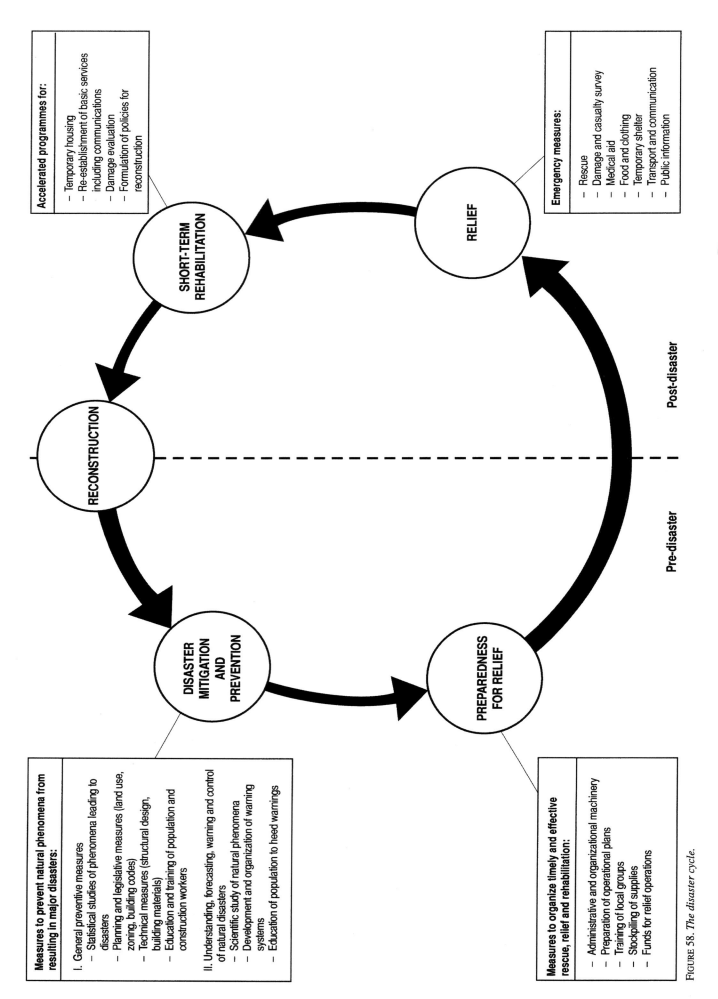

Accelerated programmes for:

  – Temporary housing
  – Re-establishment of basic services
    including communications
  – Damage evaluation
  – Formulation of policies for
    reconstruction

SHORT-TERM REHABILITATION

RECONSTRUCTION

RELIEF

Emergency measures:

  – Rescue
  – Damage and casualty survey
  – Medical aid
  – Food and clothing
  – Temporary shelter
  – Transport and communication
  – Public information

Post-disaster

Pre-disaster

DISASTER MITIGATION AND PREVENTION

PREPAREDNESS FOR RELIEF

Measures to prevent natural phenomena from resulting in major disasters:

  I. General preventive measures
    – Statistical studies of phenomena leading to
      disasters
    – Planning and legislative measures (land use,
      zoning, building codes)
    – Technical measures (structural design,
      building materials)
    – Education and training of population and
      construction workers

  II. Understanding, forecasting, warning and control
      of natural disasters
    – Scientific study of natural phenomena
    – Development and organization of warning
      systems
    – Education of population to heed warnings

Measures to organize timely and effective rescue, relief and rehabilitation:

  – Administrative and organizational machinery
  – Preparation of operational plans
  – Training of local groups
  – Stockpiling of supplies
  – Funds for relief operations

FIGURE 58. *The disaster cycle.*

- take evasive actions and/or preparedness and protective measures prior to the occurrence of disasters;
- provide immediate relief measures to save lives while protecting lifelines and vital economic assets when disasters occur; and
- institute swift and safe rehabilitation, more durable recovery and reconstruction of the society and economy so as to avoid future disasters or reduce their effects (see figure 58 opposite).

During the twentieth century, scientific, technological, policy and management innovations have significantly increased our capacity to understand various hazards, to assess risks and vulnerabilities, and to predict and provide early warning of the location and timing of disastrous events. Many natural phenomena—such as floods, avalanches, landslides and earthquakes—as well as technological installations which can cause disasters are location-specific. Even erratic phenomena such as cyclones—called hurricanes in the Americas and typhoons in South-East Asia—are known to cause most of their damage by flooding in specific locations. This suggests that evasive actions can be taken for disaster prevention and reduction, through:

- proper siting of human settlements and activities;
- appropriate land-use regulations, so that dangerous industrial plants are not located in heavily populated areas;
- building codes to ensure that structures are flood- or fire-proof or can withstand earthquakes of given intensities; and
- construction of protective installations such as dams, dikes, embankments, etc.

Although many disaster reduction measures have been developed and applied in technologically advanced societies, they have not been systematically introduced worldwide, particularly in developing countries. As human and economic losses from natural disasters have risen in recent years, those most affected tend to be the poor and socially vulnerable in developing countries. International attention is focusing on measures—appropriate to levels of industrialization, population densities and the disasters faced—which can successfully reduce the impact of disasters in developing countries, as well as the factors which affect whether or not these measures are implemented. (See box below.)

Regional priorities in reducing natural, technological and environmental disasters

The United Nations provides a range of disaster reduction services in response to requests from Governments. The needs are typically regional- or country-specific; hence DHA has organized regional, subregional and national initiatives based on the types of hazards found in the countries and their disaster management priorities. As map I on pages 4 and 5 indicates, DHA has also established three regional offices to pursue various approaches to reducing the risks of natural disasters:

- the South Pacific Programme Office (SPPO) in Suva, Fiji;
- the IDNDR Regional Office for the Americas in San Jose, Costa Rica; and
- the Regional Disaster Mitigation Office in Quito, Ecuador.

Asia and the Pacific

Asia and the Pacific is probably the region of the world most exposed to natural disasters: according to the Asian Disaster Preparedness Centre, 40 per cent of floods and 70 per cent of cyclones worldwide occur in that region. Since 1990, according to estimates of the United Nations Economic and Social Commission for Asia and the Pacific (ESCAP), natural disasters have caused over 200,000 deaths in the region. The Bangladesh cyclone of 1991 alone took about 140,000 lives and caused damage representing close to 10 per cent of the country's gross national product (GNP). The 1996 flooding in China affected 200 million people and cost more than US$ 20 billion in material losses. Two cyclones in 1990 and 1991 in Samoa caused over US$ 400 million of damage, three times the country's annual gross domestic product (GDP). Many other major disasters have occurred in the region in recent years, including the 1995 earthquake in Kobe, Japan and an earthquake in 1992 in Indonesia, followed by a tsunami, which killed several thousand people.

Asian countries are well aware of the devastating impact of natural disasters. In the aftermath of the Kobe earthquake, Japan convened in December 1995 an Asian Natural Disaster Reduction Conference, attended by ministers and delegates from 28 countries. It issued the Kobe Declaration on Natural Disaster Reduction, 1995, underscoring the importance of regional cooperation, national disaster management plans, and the involvement of local communities in all aspects of disaster management.

South Pacific

DHA's South Pacific Programme Office (SPPO) in Suva, Fiji implements a multi-faceted South Pacific Disaster Reduction Programme (SPDRP) for the benefit of 15 Pacific Island States. Established in 1992 and supported primarily by UNDP, SPPO's programmes include:

- regional- and country-specific training in the preparation of national disaster plans;
- demonstration projects for specific disaster scenarios, such as the Fiji Seismic Risk project for Suva;
- manuals for national and local governments on the "Requirements for Disaster Management in the Pacific" and "Disaster Mitigation for Planners"; and
- brochures for public education.

SPPO organizes annual meetings of national disaster managers to promote regional coordination, exchange information and review regional IDNDR work in progress.

South-East Asia

DHA activities have focused on disaster management training exercises in Myanmar, Cambodia and Laos. In Laos, DHA has also helped prepare a national disaster management strategy.

Africa

Virtually all African countries are vulnerable to natural and environmental disasters, including desertification, recurrent drought, insect infestation, bush fires and flash floods. Industrialization, uncontrolled urbanization and population growth combine to increase the likelihood of technological disasters as well. In Ethiopia, in 1991, there was an explosion in ammunition storage facilities which killed 100, injured 200 and destroyed businesses and low-income dwellings, displacing several thousand people. In Kenya, in 1993, a bridge over the Ndethai Geithia River collapsed, killing more than 200 people. In Zaire, in 1995, a plane crashed into a market near Kinshasa airport, killing 300.

DHA's current activities in Africa are based on three subregional disaster reduction workshops held in Botswana, Burkina Faso and Kenya in 1994 and 1995, following the Yokohama World Conference on Natural Disaster Reduction. The workshops engaged national authorities, the vulnerable communities and other representatives of civil society in defining problems, identifying research needs and proposing policy responses. In Madagascar, assistance was aimed at better preparedness for cyclones along the northern coast. In the aftermath of an earthquake in Uganda, technical assistance was provided on the future construction of earthquake-resistant structures and on disaster reduction management. In Botswana, Cameroon, Djibouti, Guinea, Lesotho, Malawi, Mali, Namibia and Niger, DHA has provided technical assistance to develop comprehensive disaster reduction strategies, as well as programmes to reduce the effects of specific types of disasters, such as drought, floods and infestations by insects, armyworms, quelea birds and rodents.

Latin America and the Caribbean

Earthquakes, floods, volcanic eruptions, landslides, mud slides and hurricanes are the most frequent causes of natural disasters in Latin America and the Caribbean. DHA has supported country-level multi-hazard disaster reduction programmes undertaken with counterparts from national emergency offices, civil defence organizations and training institutions.

- The DHA IDNDR Regional Office for the Americas in San José, Costa Rica, supported in part by the Pan American Health Organization (PAHO), serves countries and organizations in Latin America and the Caribbean. It runs a Regional Disaster Documentation Centre, has initiated a regional disaster information network, issues the bulletin *IDNDR Informs* and convenes regional and national conferences.
- The DHA Disaster Mitigation Regional Office in Quito, Ecuador, supports technical cooperation activities at the country level.

North/Central America

A disaster mitigation training course was conducted and a disaster mitigation project is planned in Honduras. Disaster mitigation projects are also being formulated in Mexico on earthquake damage reduction, strengthening national civil protection, and improved monitoring of the Colima and Popocatepetl volcanoes. In Guatemala, assistance is provided for protection against earthquakes, volcanic activity, landslides and floods, particularly in Guatemala City.

76

The Caribbean

Small island states are continuing natural disaster reduction efforts against seasonal hurricanes and occasional volcanic eruptions. With assistance from DHA, the Governments of Jamaica, Haiti, and Barbados are preparing country-specific disaster mitigation projects and training workshops.

South America

Activities have focused on the Andean countries. Ongoing projects on hazard and risk mapping, monitoring, emergency management, training and public awareness deal with the reduction of volcanic and industrial risks in Argentina; the reduction of volcanic risks in Chile; the reduction of disasters due to earthquakes, volcanic eruptions, floods, landslides, tsunamis and technological accidents in Colombia; disaster prevention and preparedness in relation to earthquakes, volcanic eruptions, floods, landslides, tsunamis and technological hazards in Ecuador; and the mitigation of disasters due to earthquakes, volcanic eruptions, landslides, floods, tsunamis and technological hazards in Peru. In addition, disaster mitigation workshops have been held in Paraguay and Argentina. Additional disaster mitigation projects are in preparation in Venezuela, Argentina, Paraguay, Peru and Colombia.

Newly independent and Baltic States

To promote the reduction of natural, technological and environmental disasters, DHA is supporting national initiatives to establish links between concerned institutions and to develop disaster-awareness at all levels. In Lithuania, Latvia and Belarus, national initiatives focus on snow melt, flood management and disaster reduction with support from DHA and UNDP. In Moldova, a joint DHA-UNDP project on "Strengthening Governmental Capacity for Disaster Response and Management" was launched in 1996. In Georgia, Armenia and Azerbaijan, national authorities are concentrating on the safety of important water control structures in the area, such as the Inguri dam in Georgia and Marmick dam in Armenia. DHA has assisted in the assessment of these dams and will issue a report on the projects and the needed resources. Turkmenistan, Kyrgyzstan and Kazakstan have densely populated capitals—Ashgabad, Almaty and Bishkek—which are located in areas of high seismic activity, slope instability, mudflows and floods. Thus, seismic risk reduction and emergency response management are the highest priorities. DHA has sent assessment missions to these countries and provided advice on improved disaster response and reduction. In the Russian Federation, together with the Russian Ministry for Emergency Situations (Emercom), DHA has helped organize training and exchanges between practitioners, and has participated in the work of the Inter-State Secretariat of CIS countries for disaster response and mitigation. A major recommendation of the CIS seminar held in Vladivostok in 1995 was that comprehensive disaster insurance systems be established at the country and local levels. A follow-up Regional Conference on Disaster Reduction and Insurance is now scheduled for June 1997 in St. Petersburg.

Reducing natural disasters

The United Nations has long worked with affected countries and expert communities to mitigate the effects of natural disasters. In the 1960s and early 1970s, the Centre for Housing, Building and Planning promoted natural disaster prevention in the rehabilitation and reconstruction phases of disasters. In 1972, the Office of the United Nations Disaster Relief Coordinator (UNDRO) was established. Under the terms of its founding resolution, General Assembly Resolution 2816 (1971), one of UNDRO's responsibilities, in addition to the coordination of international disaster relief, was "to promote the study, prevention, control and prediction of natural disasters, including the collection and dissemination of information concerning technological developments". In 1992, the establishment of DHA resulted in combining new responsibilities in complex emergencies with UNDRO's traditional roles in natural disaster reduction.

In addition to UNDRO, and later DHA, other programmes and specialized agencies in the United Nations system have continued to play important roles in natural disaster reduction. The UNDP, Habitat and the International Bank for Reconstruction and Development (IBRD) are all actively involved in disaster rehabilitation and reconstruction. Disaster reduction activities of WHO cover epidemics, water-borne diseases, vector control, etc. UNESCO has an active programme in the fields of seismology and volcanology, hydrology and flood control and sciences in general and their application to disaster reduction. The World Meteorological Organization (WMO) does extensive work on meteorological disasters and early warning systems for cyclones and floods. FAO has programmes dealing with hydrology and flood control, the alleviation of droughts, land erosion, pest control, food security, etc.

In 1989, as a spur for the United Nations work on natural disaster reduction, the General Assembly, in resolution 44/236, launched the International Decade for Natural Disaster Reduction (IDNDR) 1990-2000 and called for "concerted international action" to protect people from natural disasters. The Decade's overall objective is to "reduce loss of life, damage of property and the disruption of economic and social stability as a consequence of natural disasters". Through the framework of IDNDR, a cooperative global partnership has emerged among national and local governments, the research and development community, and the private sector, including banks, insurance companies, industrial enterprises, foundations and nongovernmental organizations. Convened in 138 national IDNDR committees or focal points, these partners exchange information, address policy makers, and raise awareness about reducing vulnerability to natural disasters. An advisory body of 25 experts from diverse regions and disciplines provides guidelines for national and international partners, and assesses activities carried out by organizations under the IDNDR umbrella.

The **1994 World Conference in Yokohama, Japan** was a milestone in the IDNDR process. At this midterm review, participants developed new strategies for natural disaster reduction:

- *Social sciences emphasized.* While the international scientific community spearheaded the launch of the Decade in the late 1980s, the Yokohama Conference broadened the scope of disaster mitigation work to include social science research, policy and practice. Economics, information networks and vulnerability reduction emerged as important factors in disaster reduction, warranting further exploration.
- *Public policy and media focus.* After Yokohama, many countries adopted new laws and national

FIGURE 59. *Among children's paintings exhibited at the World Conference on Natural Disaster Reduction, 1994, was 10-year-old Richmond Nitro's vision of a Filipino family made homeless by flooding.* [IDNDR]

strategies for disaster reduction, and drew public attention to them through the media.
- *Regional groupings.* As countries conducted national reviews and shared them with neighbouring countries to prepare for Yokohama, regional approaches and groupings emerged. These information and technical cooperation networks have become a high priority in the second half of IDNDR.
- *Shift from emergency preparedness to vulnerability reduction.* Many organizations at Yokohama emphasized the links between disaster reduction and sustainable development.

Since 1994, the strategy in disaster reduction has focused on disaster prevention, mitigation and preparedness, in preference to disaster response, which yields only temporary results at a very high cost. Natural disaster reduction is now not only an indispensable component of humanitarian assistance, but also a central United Nations approach to sustainable development, natural resource protection and sound environmental management.

The United Nations' current work on natural disasters is of two types: technical assistance and standard-setting in disaster reduction; and

the promotion of better policies and public awareness about disaster reduction. DHA works in any given country through the United Nations Resident Coordinator and the national IDNDR committees to integrate disaster reduction into national development planning.

Technical assistance and setting standards for disaster reduction

Successful disaster reduction management is a cyclical activity, including the five stages shown in figure 58 on page 74:
- pre-disaster preventive and mitigating actions;
- formulation of emergency plans and preparedness activities;
- disaster relief interventions;
- short-term recovery and rehabilitation;
- longer-term reconstruction.

To be effective, these stages must integrate research and development, information exchange, capacity-building and training, and the implementation of appropriate solutions in vulnerable communities. DHA addresses these various stages of disaster reduction management by:
- sponsoring specialized fellowships;
- producing specialized technical publications for researchers, policy makers and the public on such

issues as hazard mapping, risk and vulnerability assessment, legal and economic aspects of disaster reduction, and the use of economic and fiscal incentives for disaster reduction purposes;

- organizing subregional, national and local workshops and seminars for government officials, researchers, community residents and NGOs; and
- developing strategies, programmes and projects for efficient disaster reduction in specific circumstances, in response to official national requests.

Improving policies and public awareness about disaster reduction

Improved policies. The IDNDR Secretariat works with the United Nations system, national and local governments, the research and development community, NGOs and the private business sector to advocate improved policies for disaster reduction.

Working with other parts of the United Nations, the IDNDR Secretariat has:

- ensured that disaster reduction policies were on the agenda of the 1994 Global Conference on the Sustainable Development of Small Island Developing States;
- been designated ''task manager'' for natural disaster reduction issues by the Commission for Sustainable Development; and
- presented proposals for urban disaster mitigation that were incorporated in the final document of the 1996 Second United Nations Conference on Human Settlements, Habitat II.

Working with national and local governments, the IDNDR Secretariat has:

- launched the RADIUS project to help urban areas worldwide cope

with earthquakes and seismic activity. Films and manuals on seismic risk assessment are being developed to help local authorities do contingency planning. Ten urban areas are being selected for case studies of earthquake damage scenarios, with a view to assessing and reducing the cities' vulnerability to earthquakes; and

- sponsored studies and developed manuals for national and local authorities on how lending and financial institutions might use certain economic instruments— mortgage and other loans, grants and subsidies, tax and financial incentives and insurance—to ensure local compliance with land use regulations and building codes.

Working with the research and development community, the IDNDR Secretariat:

- organized working groups on early warning related to geophysical, hydro-meteorological and technological hazards, communications technology, and local and national applications preparatory to a 1998 international conference on early warning to be convened by IDNDR and the Government of Germany;
- initiated a worldwide effort to collect data on the cost of natural disasters in terms of physical destruction, lost income and production, relief operations and the additional costs of providing basic services, so as to facilitate meaningful cost-benefit studies;
- endorsed and monitored 60 IDNDR demonstration projects carried out by national and international bodies, universities and researchers to develop best practices in disaster reduction; and
- with the University of Geneva and UNESCO, is establishing the University Information Network for Disaster Reduction, which will

provide an electronic database and web site for institutions engaged in various aspects of natural disaster reduction.

Working with the private sector, the IDNDR Secretariat has:

- joined IBM-Business Recovery Services in launching in March 1997 a new ''Leadership Coalition for Global Business Protection''. The coalition brings together Governments, business firms and associations, as well as NGOs to promote hazard awareness and appropriate corporate asset management practices in both the private and public sectors; and
- supported the activities of the NGO Forum for Disaster Reduction, which held its first global meeting, following the Yokohama Conference, in Kathmandu in October 1996.

Public awareness. The IDNDR secretariat also promoted public awareness about natural disaster reduction. It has launched:

- the World Disaster Reduction Day Campaigns: annual, theme-oriented campaigns to create interest in disaster mitigation and reduction and highlight their links to environmental and development practices. The 1996 campaign, on Cities at Risk, underscored the increasing vulnerability of cities to natural disasters and identified practical ways to mitigate this vulnerability. (See figure 60 overleaf and box on Protecting cities at risk, page 81.)
- *Stop Disasters*, a quarterly magazine published by the International Stop Disasters Institute in Naples, Italy. The magazine, with an overall circulation of 20,000 copies in six languages, includes articles on human settlements, early warning, environment and civil protection.

Making Cities Safer...*before* disaster strikes

FIGURE 60. *Poster issued for the 1996 Cities at Risk Awareness Campaign launched by IDNDR.*

Protecting cities at risk

Nearly half of the world's population now lives in urban areas and 80 per cent of population growth in the 1990s is taking place in urban areas. In developing countries, this trend is even stronger. By the year 2000, 17 of the 20 largest cities in the world will be in the developing world, compared with seven in 1950.

Many of these mega-cities are in areas where floods, earthquakes, landslides and other potentially disastrous events are likely to occur. With rapid urban growth, it is more difficult to provide basic infrastructure, suitable land, well-constructed buildings, and safe storage and disposal of hazardous materials.

The 1996 World Disaster Reduction Campaign focused on "Cities at Risk" to encourage better policies about and greater public awareness of urban disasters and their mitigation. Through the IDNDR Secretariat, DHA worked with national and local governments, associations of cities, universities, NGOs and private firms in 65 countries in a world campaign.

- A policy report, *Cities at Risk*, outlined case studies, policy options and contacts which organizations could adapt for their own purposes.
- An Internet conference, *Solutions for Cities at Risk,* provided extensive networking among about 450 participants and a forum for global debate on eight specific topics related to urban disaster mitigation. The parallel World Wide Web site attracted about 82,000 visits in the two-month conference period. Participants could assess contributions and follow up on subjects as diverse as social vulnerability in Tokyo, early warning and telecommunications issues in western Canada, and community participation techniques for fire prevention in Australia.

Many national and regional organizations are now carrying out activities to ensure that disaster preparedness becomes an integral part of all urban development planning and of all environmental impact assessments.

Reducing technological disasters

Various industries and fields of activity often have their own safety regulations which can prevent the occurrence or reduce the effects of technological disasters. When these systems fail, or are inadequate, results can be catastrophic. Since 1992, DHA has been the United Nations focal point for coordinating the international response to one such tragic industrial accident: the 1986 explosion of the Chernobyl nuclear reactor in the then Ukrainian SSR (see box on Chernobyl, overleaf).

At the same time, several United Nations agencies have been engaged in reducing the incidence and effects of technological disasters by promoting good practices in their respective areas. Thus, the International Labour Organisation (ILO), WHO, the United Nations Industrial Development Organization (UNIDO), the International Atomic Energy Agency (IAEA), UNESCO, the International Maritime Organization (IMO) and the International Civil Aviation Organization (ICAO) all have activities related to the prevention of industrial, maritime or air accidents. In addition, IMO and IAEA have programmes to prevent or mitigate the environmental damage of marine pollution and radioactivity, respectively. Many other kinds of environmental damage caused by technological or industrial accidents, however, remained without a consistent and assured source of assistance in the United Nations system.

Resolution 44/236, which created IDNDR, emphasized in its preamble "that appropriate emergency planning for natural disasters and its integration in national development plans could also be very helpful in preventing . . . other kinds of disasters, such as those of an industrial or technological nature." At the 1994 Yokohama Conference, participants concluded that "the concept of disaster reduction should be enlarged to cover natural and other disaster situations including environmental and technological disasters" and recommended the "adoption of integrated policies for prevention of, prepared-ness for, and response to, natural disasters and other disaster situations including environmental and technological hazards."[2]

Increased industrialization especially in developing countries has caused an increasing number of accidents. This, in turn, has increased the environmental consciousness of the international community and triggered a range of international environmental assistance programmes. While the wide variety of possible technological and other man-made disasters precludes adopting a single set of safety precautions, DHA and the United Nations Environment Programme (UNEP) have been mandated to improve the international response to environmental emergencies. Having established a Joint UNEP/DHA Environment Unit in 1994, the two United Nations bodies have begun to address the environmental consequences of such

---

[2] *Yokohama Strategy and Plan of Action for a Safer World*, United Nations, 1994, pp. 8-9.

disasters as chemical and oil spills, industrial accidents, forest fires and other sudden-onset emergencies that cause, or threaten, environmental damage and which can have serious impacts on human health and welfare.

The Joint Unit is financed primarily by UNEP and organizationally lodged in DHA, which provides it with both office support and emergency response facilities. The Unit carries out a range of activities, including independent assessments of environmental emergencies upon the request of governments. UNEP and DHA have set up an open-ended International Advisory Group on Environmental Emergencies to bring together national experts and focal points from countries around the world. The Advisory Group meets annually to share experiences in the field of response to environmental disasters, to review the work of the Joint Unit, and to provide advice and guidance on its future activities.

THE CHERNOBYL DISASTER

In the early morning of Saturday, 26 April 1986, two explosions blew the roof off Unit 4 of the Chernobyl nuclear power plant in the then Ukrainian SSR, just north of Kiev. The explosion exposed the reactor core to the atmosphere and led to the largest short-term release of radioactive materials from one source ever recorded. Hot gases, smoke and radioactive materials were carried almost two kilometres into the night sky, to be subsequently swept by prevailing winds throughout western parts of the USSR, to eastern and western Europe (see map VIII, page 84). In the Soviet Union alone, over 4 million people were exposed to significant levels of radiation.

The release of large quantities of radioactive material continued over the 10-day period that it took the 800,000 rescue workers and military personnel—who became known as the "liquidators"—to bring the reactor fire under control. Changing wind conditions and sporadic rainfall resulted in a very uneven and complex pattern of radioactive fall-out over vast regions. Levels dangerous enough to necessitate the relocation of populations were found as far away as 200 kilometres from the accident site. The disaster ultimately displaced some 400,000 people in the three most affected countries—Belarus, the Russian Federation and Ukraine—and has had a devastating impact upon the subregion's economy and environment.

While refugees and internally displaced persons who flee their homes due to conflict can generally hope to return someday, many people displaced by Chernobyl will never be able to go home. Their communities will be contaminated by radionuclides for centuries. The threat of future, personal disaster hangs over Chernobyl's survivors. There is ample cause for concern. Thyroid cancers, for example, have already increased 285 times over the pre-Chernobyl levels and are not expected to peak until 2005-2010. Increased incidence of other cancers which can be linked to the disaster have long incubation periods and have not yet been recorded. The "liquidators" have already experienced higher morbidity rates, while illness rates among inhabitants of mildly contaminated areas are higher than those of the overall population.

Stress-related diseases are also on the increase among the affected populations, in addition to the somatic problems. When one imagines coping with an enemy that is invisible, that may hide in the ground, in the water or in the food, the emergence of such diseases can begin to be understood. Economic hardship has often forced people to forage for food in clearly contaminated areas, or to rely on suspect goods obtained on the black market.

The manner and content of the initial response from the Soviet authorities left a legacy of scepticism as to the facts, and a loss of confidence among the affected populations. Indeed it was not until 1990 that the Soviet Union brought an appeal for assistance before the United Nations. The resulting General Assembly resolution 45/190 of 21 December 1990 led to the establishment of a United Nations inter-agency task force and a Coordinator of International Cooperation on Chernobyl, a post subsequently assigned to the Under-Secretary-General for Humanitarian Affairs shortly after the establishment of DHA. An international appeal for contributions to the United Nations Chernobyl Trust Fund at a Pledging Conference in September 1991, generated less than US$ 1 million, although in the two subsequent years approximately US$ 20 million was channelled to agencies in the task force, primarily for health-related projects. An equivalent amount was also provided to the three affected countries bilaterally, although this was principally used to enhance nuclear safety. Even this relatively modest support from the international community has, due to a lack of appreciation of the persistent nature of the Chernobyl problem, largely petered out.

Within these resource constraints, the United Nations system has attempted to address the urgent needs of those most affected by Chernobyl by:

- providing proper medical diagnosis and treatment of Chernobyl-related conditions;
- securing adequate supplies of drugs for the growing number of victims whose thyroid glands have been surgically removed;
- meeting mental health needs; and
- treating stress-related illnesses.

In 1996, on the tenth anniversary of the accident, a number of international conferences were held: the WHO International Conference on the Health Consequences of the Chernobyl and other radiological accidents; the International Conference of the EU, Belarus, the Russian Federation and Ukraine on the radiological consequences of the Chernobyl accident; and an IAEA-WHO-EU Conference in cooperation with DHA, UNESCO, UNEP and others on One Decade After Chernobyl. The results of these conferences clearly pointed to the need for intensifying assistance to vast segments of the populations of the affected states, as well as to the need for further research.

In its continuing attempt to assist the affected populations, to understand the complex pattern of damage, and to revitalize the interest of governments in this largely forgotten disaster, and on the recommendation of the Governments of Belarus, the Russian Federation and Ukraine, in May 1997 DHA will send an inter-agency mission to the affected regions of the three countries. The team will assess current needs and recommend continued assistance by the international community to alleviate immediate human suffering and help cope with Chernobyl's long-term effects.

The mission's report will also be presented at the DHA-sponsored International Seminar on ''Chernobyl and Beyond: Humanitarian Assistance to Victims of Technological Disasters'', scheduled in Moscow from 27-28 May 1997, in cooperation with the Ministry for Emergency Situations of the Russian Federation (EMERCOM). The Seminar, will bring together international aid organizations, Governments, scientists, lawyers, academicians and the media, to develop an overall assistance strategy for implementation by the international community. It will also outline a methodology for addressing the life-cycle of a technological disaster, ranging from the prior risk reduction measures that can be taken, to assessing the specific needs of those affected when a disaster strikes, through to the response itself: its financing and mechanisms for effective coordination.

In conclusion . . . prospects for future disaster mitigation and reduction hinge upon the extent to which all levels in society succeed in ''mainstreaming'' the issue: developing systematic policies and programmes that incorporate protection from disaster risks. In order to be successful, disaster reduction techniques must be known, accepted and practised by governments, private business organizations, other private organizations and vulnerable communities throughout the world.

The IDNDR process and the conclusions of the Yokohama Conference have identified the key partners and mechanisms at the local, national, regional and international levels. IDNDR will continue to encourage an open-ended, participatory process, in order to assess remaining gaps and propose effective disaster reduction initiatives beyond the year 2000. The challenge for the United Nations is to facilitate action by all concerned to ensure that a culture of prevention is maintained and strengthened by the time IDNDR officially ends in the year 2000 ∎

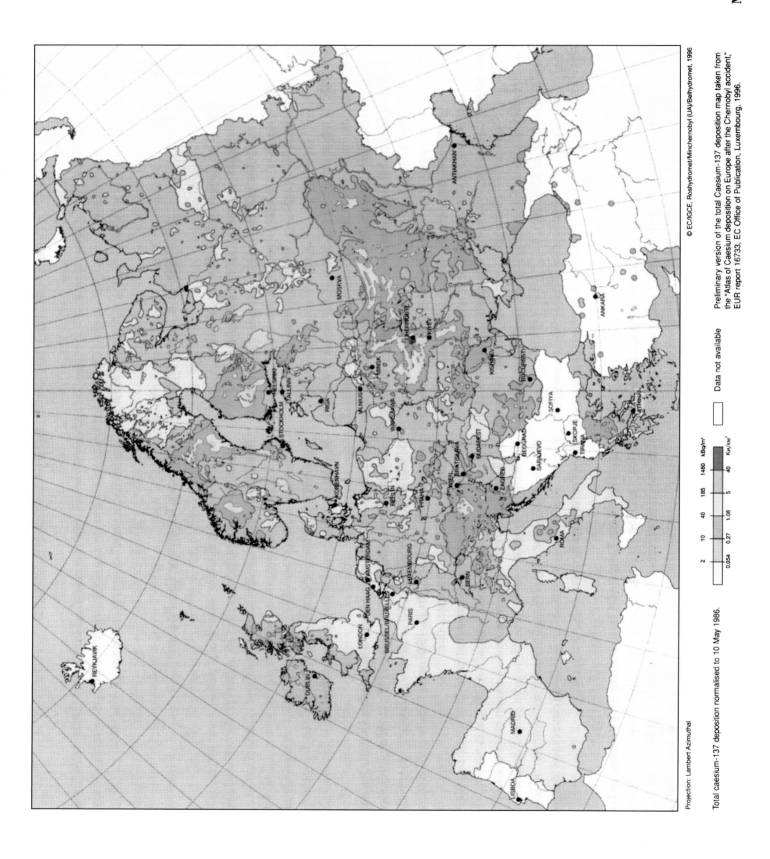

MAP VIII

Projection: Lambert Azimuthal

Total caesium-137 deposition normalised to 10 May 1986.

© EC/IGCE, Roshydromet/Minchernobyl (UA)/Belhydromet, 1996

Preliminary version of the total Caesium-137 deposition map taken from the "Atlas of Caesium deposition on Europe after the Chernobyl accident," EUR report 16733, EC Office of Publication, Luxembourg, 1996.

						kBq/m²
2	10	40	185	1480		
0.054	0.27	1.08	5	40		Ku/км²

Data not available

Communicating through Art

2. Draw a Disaster That Could Happen to Your Community

In April 1994, government officials of Petropavlosky (a city in eastern Russia) announced that Koryacksky Volcano, 25 km away, was about to erupt. Below are some paintings drawn by children from Petropavlosky, 10 days after the announcement.

For you and your classmates

Think of the maps you used earlier in this booklet. What kind of disaster may strike your area? Draw what might happen if you are not prepared.

Clockwise from top left: Disobedient Volcano Koryackscky – Svetlana Chekutova, 13 years old; Beautifully and Unmercifully – Anna Kazantseva, 13 years old; Fiery River – Karina Pack, 10 years old; Angry Volcano – Katya Grechanyuck, 13 years old. Children's Art School Number 1, Petropavlosky, Russia.
Shown at the World Conference on Natural Disaster Reduction, Yokohama, Japan, 1994.

FIGURE 61. *A selection of paintings by Russian schoolchildren, depicting the eruption of a local volcano.* [IDNDR, *Learning about Natural Disasters*, 1995]

Chapter 11

The global scourge of anti-personnel landmines

FIGURE 62. *Afghanistan: some mine-clearance techniques, such as manual prodding, are virtually the same as those used 50 years ago.*

The presence of uncleared anti-personnel landmines (AP mines) and unexploded ordnance (UXO) in areas needed for human settlement and economic activity is among the world's most serious humanitarian problems. More than 60 countries are affected. (See map XI, pages 94 and 95.)

AP mines kill or injure indiscriminately. Victims are usually civilians, killed or injured after hostilities have come to an end. The ICRC estimates that throughout the world, every month some 800 people are killed and another 1,200 maimed as a result of accidents with landmines and UXOs: about one victim every 20 minutes.

The impacts of landmines and unexploded ordnance extend far beyond individual casualties; they are a major impediment to post-conflict reconstruction and development, particularly in mine-affected developing countries where economic activity is still centered on agriculture. In many cases, landmines have been laid to prevent the use and rehabilitation of

farmland, bridges, roads, and water supply facilities. After a conflict ends, landmines—or even the perceived threat of landmines—can pose significant obstacles to the resettlement of refugees and internally displaced persons. In the longer-term, by denying people access to

their land, landmines are a significant factor in the impoverishment of entire communities. In some areas of Cambodia, for example, landmines deployed during the 18-year-long civil war rendered over 50 per cent of the cultivable area inaccessible. In addition to causing severe physical injuries, landmines also cause psychological trauma. The already weak health-care systems in war-torn societies are faced with the need to invest scarce resources in complicated surgeries, long hospital stays and expensive prosthetic and rehabilitation services. If they do not, mine victims and their families—often from the poorest sectors of society—are left to cope on their own with the life-long medical and socio-economic consequences of mine injuries.

Since AP mines and UXOs retain their lethal capacity for decades, their humanitarian impact also will continue for decades, unless they are systematically addressed at the earliest opportunity. Yet mine-clearance, given currently available technologies, is slow, costly, labour-intensive and risky, and more cost-effective technologies are only slowly becom-

FIGURE 63. *Rwanda: a landmine can be hidden in potholes in a road.*

ing available for humanitarian application. Overall estimates for the total cost of clearing the world's landmines with current technologies run into billions of dollars.

It is important to recognize, however, that while landmines, unexploded ordnance and other debris of war litter vast areas, not all present an immediate threat. Mine-infested land which is either uninhabited or uninhabitable may, for example, remain uncleared without posing undue risk. Properly targeted national humanitarian mine-clearance programmes—such as in Cambodia—can quickly have a significant impact in liberating productive land and reducing casualties.

FIGURE 65. *Mozambique: one of the initial activities in demining operations is the identification and clear marking of minefields.*

United Nations humanitarian mine action: principles

The United Nations system, together with Member States, the ICRC, and several dedicated non-governmental organizations, have helped establish mine action programmes throughout the world. In September 1994, the United Nations Secretary-General designated DHA as the United Nations focal point for all demining and landmine-related issues with a view to fostering an integrated and coordinated approach to address this problem. At the same time, the Secretary-General set up a Voluntary Trust Fund for Assistance in Mine-Clearance.

DHA is mandated to "develop more formal working arrangements with all parties in order to outline more clearly the role each agency will play in the provision of assistance in mine clearance."[1] To achieve this, DHA has put forward the following principles or guidelines, as a starting point in clarifying these individual roles:

- Action to address the mine problem must begin as early as

[1] *Report of the Secretary-General to the General Assembly*, A/50/408, 6 September 1995.

possible. In the event of an ongoing crisis or conflict in which AP mines play a significant part, information-gathering, advocacy, mine-awareness and medical issues should be pursued even before the peace process begins.

- During negotiations to end the conflict, the peace process should set out the political and organizational framework needed to begin a mine action programme, once the security and political situation permits.
- In addition to mine-clearance in accordance with agreed standards and priorities, a mine action plan must encompass mine-awareness; risk reduction and education; capacity building; and treatment of mine casualties, including their rehabilitation.
- Comparative advantage should apply, so that elements of the plan are carried out by those most capable and available to do so.

Priorities for United Nations mine-clearance

A distinction has sometimes been made between humanitarian mine-clearance and mine-clearance for development/reconstruction.[2] In many

[2] See *The Priority Reconstruction Program: From Emergency to Sustainability,* World Bank, November 1996.

FIGURE 64. *Mozambique: even the presumed presence of landmines can lead to a protracted dislocation of village populations.*

cases, however, the links between various aspects of a country's recovery—reintegration of refugees and IDPs, revival of communities, reconstruction—are such that there is considerable overlap and no clear distinction. For example, clearing mines to rehabilitate housing in a village to which refugees are to return is a mix of support for resettlement and reconstruction, but with a significant humanitarian impact. It is important, therefore, that specific priorities be established through inter-agency and government consultations, although recognizing that the highest priority should be given to clearing mines which present a direct threat to human life. A typical set of priorities for humanitarian mine action—adopted by the Cambodia mine action plan—could be as follows:[3]

_____

[3] See *Cambodia Mine Action Centre (CMAC) Five-Year Strategy: May 1996 to December 2000.*

FIGURE 67. *Angola: ingenious application of existing technologies can increase the safety and speed of demining high-risk areas.*

Priority 1: providing emergency access for the delivery of humanitarian aid and land for the resettlement and rehabilitation of IDPs and refugees;

Priority 2: clearing occupied, contaminated land in which a high casualty rate is being experienced;

Priority 3: clearing land for agriculture;

Priority 4: clearing land for community development needs, e.g. schools, places of worship, hospitals, etc.; and

Priority 5: clearing land for reconstruction and development projects.

The issue of capacity building

The primary responsibility for taking action against the presence of mines lies with the concerned state. Where, as is often the case, local capacity to demine is lacking and must be developed, the United Nations will assist in creating a local capacity that can continue once direct support through the United Nations has ended. Mine-clearance is a necessary task in its own right, however, and capacity building is not an end in itself. There is little merit in training more and more deminers if the task can be

accomplished more effectively and faster by other means. The balance between capacity building and rapid, efficient demining must clearly be in favour of the latter. Therefore, as the appropriate technologies mature, reliance on the current slow, high-risk, labour-intensive methods of demining must be reduced or eliminated entirely, and local capacity developed to utilize the new technologies.

DHA role in humanitarian demining

In its capacity as the designated United Nations focal point for mine action, DHA cannot and does not carry out the complex range of actions required to address the mine problem on its own. Based on its mandate, the previously elaborated principles and its experience in field operations, the DHA role can be broken into four stages: planning and assessment; initiating the mine action programme; consolidating and executing the programme; and transferring or terminating the programme. (These four stages in the largest DHA mine action programme in Bosnia and Herzegovina are described in the box following.)

FIGURE 66. *Afghanistan: the loss of a leg for a child often means a life of dependency and hardship.* [UNICEF/92-136/John Isaac]

A summary of mine action activities in Bosnia and Herzegovina: 1996-early 1997

Hundreds of thousands of anti-personnel landmines and unexploded ordnance remain a threat throughout Bosnia and Herzegovina (BH), especially along the former confrontation lines. As many as 600 civilians are reported to have been killed by landmines in BH in 1996. In addition to actual mine incidents, the perception in the minds of local people that an area is mined actually prevents its use for resettlement and the resumption of normal activities, particularly in agricultural areas.

Casualties from landmines in BH

Civilians

ICRC records from the first 11 months of 1996 contain information on some 312 landmine victims, 193 from the Federation and 119 in the Republika Srpska. Because the ICRC introduced the programme in a phased manner, and was not able to collect data in all areas of BH in 1996, the data are not complete.

It is estimated that the overall casualty rate in BH is 50 per month. Recent information indicates that there were 102 casualties in the Sarajevo area alone in 1996. (See map X, page 92.) More comprehensive data will be forthcoming in the near future as data-gathering is conducted on an on-going basis. Using a 1996 sample of 604 households in BH:

- 80 per cent of casualties are male;
- most of the male casualties are farmers returning to their land.

I-FOR

In 1996, the Implementation Force suffered 77 casualties, including:

- 10 persons killed;
- 20 persons seriously injured;
- 47 persons with minor injuries.

Following the November 1995 Dayton-Paris Peace Agreement, DPKO, UNHCR and UNICEF, together with the Implementation Force (I-FOR), ICRC and some international NGOs, began to address the problems of mine-clearance in order to carry out their peace-keeping and humanitarian missions. In February 1996, DPKO, in conjunction with the Government of the United States, established the Mine Action Centre (MAC) as part of the United Nations Mission in Bosnia and Herzegovina (UNMIBH). Once initial mine-clearance was completed, and in order to address the longer-term humanitarian, rehabilitation and reconstruction priorities, in June 1996, DPKO handed the MAC over to DHA, with UNMIBH continuing to provide administrative support.

Development of the mine action programme

The Government of Bosnia and Herzegovina has the responsibility for defining and implementing an integrated mine action programme that serves the needs of the country as a whole. DHA's role is to provide expert assistance, drawing on the experience of the international community in developing and implementing such programmes elsewhere. The MAC's major objective is to help the Government develop local capacity to deal with the mine problem.

Initially, the MAC was intended to serve in a purely coordinating and advisory role, while utilizing local capacity to execute the major operational components of the programme:

- Surveying and marking of minefields;
- Clearance of anti-personnel (AP) mines and unexploded ordnance (UXO);
- Explosive Ordnance Disposal (EOD); and
- Mine-Awareness Programmes.

By September 1996, it was clear that only very limited local capacity existed to handle these tasks and, as a result, the MAC accepted a greater responsibility for various components of the programme.

The MAC created a national headquarters in Sarajevo, with regional offices in Mostar, Tuzla, Bihac and Banja Luka, to collect information, coordinate and monitor ongoing activities and ensure that international standards are maintained. The MAC works closely with organizations involved in funding and/or implementing mine-clearance projects in BH—including UNESCO, UNICEF, the World Bank, the European Union (EU), the ICRC, NGOs such as Handicap International and Norwegian People's Aid (NPA), and international and local commercial companies. Since June 1996 the MAC has:

- Developed a mines database with information on mines, survey results, clearance records, and mine casualties. The database can generate maps of mined areas and help planners focus on the most important priorities;

Landmines data for BH: 1996

- Of an estimated 60 per cent of BH land surveyed, there are 17,483 minefields.
- These minefields contain an estimated 221,000 mines.

Of these mined areas:

- 300 minefields contain more than 100 mines per minefield;
- 12,000 minefields contain less than 10 mines per minefield;
- Over 2,000 minefields have been cleared, primarily by the former warring factions, but also by international and local commercial companies.

- Launched training programmes for mine-clearance and other technical personnel. Training will begin in May 1997 throughout the country, and actual mine-clearance will begin in June 1997. Initial targets are the training of three demining teams, totalling 120 personnel, as well as three minefield marking teams;

- Promoted mine-awareness programmes by making minefield marking supplies available to civil defence units, and training minefield marking teams for rapid response in emergencies;
- Allocated almost US$ 2 million for small-scale mine-clearance contracts and the development of local mine-clearance capacity; and
- Developed a National Mine Action Plan for 1997, in coordination with the National Commission on Demining, as well as with regional authorities.

The Government of Bosnia and Herzegovina has formed a National Commission on Demining with representation from the Federation and the Republika Srpska, which will implement the mine programme in their respective entities. Although local operational capacity for demining activities still remains negligible in comparison with the scale of the problem, substantial progress has been made on the National Mine Action Plan, particularly since the London Conference agreements in December 1996. Only by developing a standing national mine-clearance capacity that will be available to the Government of Bosnia and Herzegovina over time can there be a sustainable solution to the extensive problems posed by mines contamination. The MAC is scheduled to hand over the programme to the BH authorities by the end of 1997.

Funding of the MAC: 1996-1997

Between 1 June and 31 December 1996, DHA spent US$ 700,000 from the Voluntary Trust Fund to develop the MAC. An additional US$ 6.8 million was received for the period January-April 1997, enabling the MAC to start developing national infrastructure. The United Nations intends to support the development of a national mine-clearance capacity in BH, with other donors supporting other aspects of the National Mine Action Plan.

Donor involvement in humanitarian demining in BH: 1997

Existing and/or planned mine action projects for BH, by donor:

World Bank:

Developing capacity of a local contractor in Olivo, involving 40 local and international supervisory staff, and supporting survey and minefield marking projects, mine-awareness activities and mine-clearance work that facilitates reconstruction.

The United States of America:

Establishing small training facilities at Brus and Mostar, teams of 90 mine-clearers and 75 surveyors with 31 mine survey dogs. The US Government's humanitarian programme will conclude in May 1997 and transfer its assets to the National Commission on Demining.

The European Union:

Establishing 18 mine-clearance teams and nine explosive ordnance disposal teams supported by international supervisory staff and the purchase of equipment. The EU is planning to train local staff to take responsibility for managing this capacity by July 1997.

Norwegian People's Aid (NPA):

Established a small training facility in Tuzla, and is planning a training facility for demining dogs in Mostar. Currently deploys 100 trained deminers and a mechanized clearance capability.

Stabilization Force (S-FOR):

Engaging in mine information and clearance activities, providing personnel for the MAC, and training and equipping 450 members of former warring factions for mine-clearance activities, in close cooperation with the US Department of State.

LANDMINE RISK AS OF JUNE 1996

Map No. 3994 UNITED NATIONS
May 1997

Department of Public Information
Cartographic Secton

MAP IX

LANDMINE INCIDENTS IN SARAJEVO (JUNE 1992-SEPTEMBER 1996)

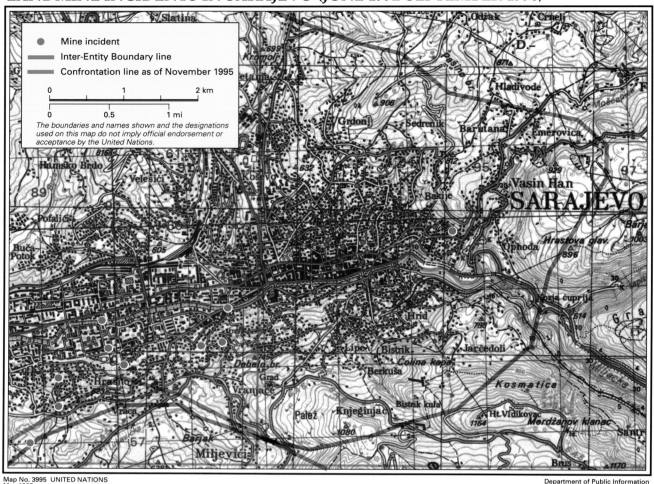

- ●   Mine incident
- ▬▬   Inter-Entity Boundary line
- ▬▬   Confrontation line as of November 1995

0   1   2 km

0   0.5   1 mi

The boundaries and names shown and the designations used on this map do not imply official endorsement or acceptance by the United Nations.

Map No. 3995   UNITED NATIONS
May 1997

Department of Public Information
Cartographic Secton

MAP X

Planning and assessment. DHA is fully engaged in the planning and preparation of new humanitarian mine action programmes. With representation appropriate to the emergency at hand, a team or teams will be formed to conduct assessment missions and prepare an implementation plan. If a mine action programme is being transferred from a peace-keeping or other mission, DHA plans and facilitates the transfer.

Initiating the mine action programme. DHA establishes the mechanisms for coordination, including a Mine Action Centre (MAC) with primary responsibility for coordinating the entire mine effort in the affected country. DHA mobilizes the resources necessary to initiate the programme: utilizing ex-

isting stand-by personnel to run the programme in country, in-kind contributions from donors, and funds from the Voluntary Trust Fund for Assistance in Mine-Clearance.

Consolidating and executing the programme. In principle, DHA does not itself execute a programme on the ground unless absolutely necessary. It will work out the best division of responsibilities among the operational organizations, taking into account their comparative advantages and in-country capacity. For example, UNHCR, UNICEF and ICRC have conducted mine-awareness training and risk reduction education; WFP and UNHCR have initiated mine-clearance programmes; and UNDP and UNOPS have administered a range of programmes at the field level. As peace building proceeds,

local authorities may begin to take more control of the operation, while DHA's involvement declines to one of coordination and policy. Funding for this phase comes directly from donors, through the United Nations Consolidated Inter-Agency Appeal process.

Transferring or terminating the programme. The goal of any mine action programme is to build local capacity to such a point that the host government can take full responsibility. Beforehand, DHA ensures that all elements of the programme are in place, that priorities have been negotiated and established, and that the programme is being executed as efficiently and effectively as possible. Where such a transfer is not practical, the United Nations programme con-

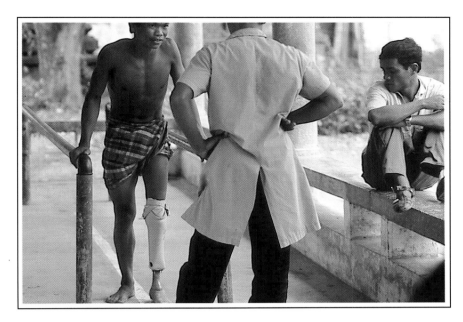

FIGURE 68. *Cambodia: the international community is slowly addressing the needs of mine survivors.* [UNICEF/92-437/Roger Lemoyne]

tinues as long as there remains a need and sufficient external funding.

The Voluntary Trust Fund for Assistance in Mine-Clearance

The Voluntary Trust Fund for Assistance in Mine-Clearance can be drawn upon at any time for:

- conduct of assessment missions to determine the scope of a mine-related problem;
- establishment and support of local Mine Action Centres and indigenous capacities;
- conduct of priority surveys, mine-awareness, training and mine-clearance operations;
- bridging of delays in funding within existing programmes;
- coordination of the international mine effort;
- collection, collation and dissemination of mine-related information of a technical nature; and
- consciousness-raising through public information.

Since the Fund was set up in November 1994, approximately US$ 31 million has been received and US$ 6.5 million pledged by almost 40 Member States and various organizations. The ten largest contributors have been: the European Union, Japan, Denmark, the United States of America, Switzerland, Germany, Norway, Italy, Sweden and the United Kingdom. As of April 1997, more than US$ 29 million has been spent or committed for expenditure on mine action programmes in Bosnia and Herzegovina, Angola, Mozambique, Croatia/ Eastern Slavonia, Afghanistan, Laos and Yemen, as well as on studies, conferences and other operating costs.

Towards a global ban on anti-personnel landmines

Over the past two years, there has been clear progress in the coordination of humanitarian mine-clearance activities, especially at the field level. No matter what progress is made in mobilizing these various institutions to address the global landmines threat, however, mine-clearance alone cannot and will not solve the landmines problem. It is equally important to pursue efforts to proceed towards a total ban on the production, stockpiling, transfer and use of anti-personnel landmines. As the United Nations focal point for mine action, DHA works with the ICRC and many NGOs—including the International Coalition to Ban Land-mines—in support of this goal.

There is a growing recognition by the international community that AP mines are an unacceptable weapon. The Secretary-General has urged all States to ensure the early entry into force of amended Protocol II to the 1980 United Nations Convention on Prohibitions or Restrictions on the Use of Certain Conventional Weapons. He has also expressed appreciation for the 78 Member States which have made unilateral declarations or adopted national measures to curb the transfer or production of landmines, as steps leading to the ultimate elimination of these weapons. The Ottawa International Strategy Conference of 3-5 October 1996 has also further stimulated support

FIGURE 69. *Cambodia: this child will need successive prosthetic devices before reaching adulthood.* [UNICEF/92-389/Roger Lemoyne]

MAP XI

UNITED NATIONS
LANDMINE PROGRAMMES
1 June 1994 - 31 March 1997

DENMARK

NETHERLANDS
BELGIUM   GERMANY
LUXEMBURG
                 AUSTRIA
                 SLOVENIA
                 CROATIA
                 BOSI
                 HERZEGO

TUNIS

LIB
AR
JAMA

Western
Sahara

MAURITANIA

SENEGAL

GUATEMALA   HONDURAS

EL SALVADOR   NICARAGUA
   COSTA RICA

LIBERIA

COLOMBIA

ECUADOR

ANC

PERU

NAM

Falkland Is.
(Malvinas)

○ UN landmine programmes

Mine-affected country
or territory

Map No. 4005   UNITED NATIONS
May 1997

Department of Public Information
Cartographic Section

94

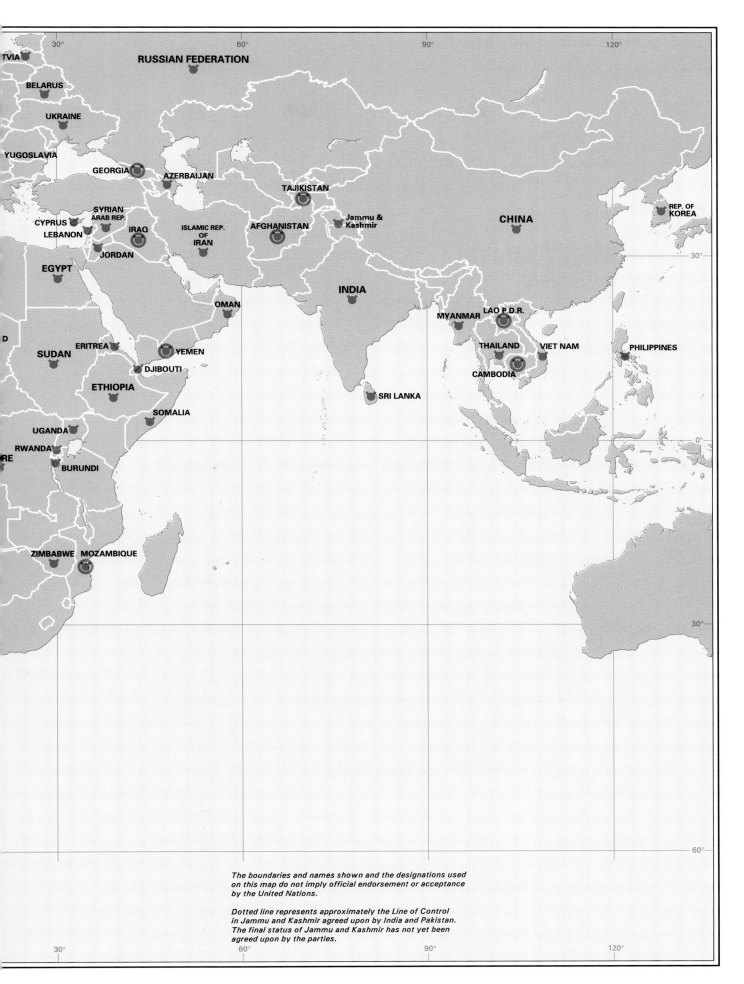

The boundaries and names shown and the designations used on this map do not imply official endorsement or acceptance by the United Nations.

Dotted line represents approximately the Line of Control in Jammu and Kashmir agreed upon by India and Pakistan. The final status of Jammu and Kashmir has not yet been agreed upon by the parties.

for a total ban: winning wide endorsement from the United Nations General Assembly in resolution 51/45S (1996). This so-called Ottawa Process is to be continued at a conference in Brussels in June 1997 and has the goal of inviting States to sign a treaty on a ban on AP mines by the end of 1997. To date, more than 60 countries have indicated their willingness to support the Ottawa Process. In Geneva, the Committee on Disarmament also has an AP mines ban under consideration.

While progress towards a ban on AP mines will be determined in these inter-governmental fora, DHA will continue to network, support international conferences, and make information available to Member States and others concerned with this important issue (see box below)■

FIGURE 70. *Afghanistan: demining operations are increasingly utilizing trained dogs, whose acute sense of smell enables them to detect explosives and plastics.*

Major conferences towards a global ban on landmines

Intergovernmental conferences

3 May 1996
Third Session of the Review Conference of the States Parties to the Convention on Conventional Weapons (CCW)
Geneva, Switzerland

3-5 October 1996
International Strategy Conference: Towards a Global Ban on Anti-Personnel Mines
Ottawa, Ontario, Canada

19-21 May 1997
Towards A Mine-free Africa: The OAU and the Legacy of Anti-Personnel Mines
Kempton Park, South Africa

2-4 December 1997
International Strategy Conference: Towards a Global Ban on Anti-Personnel Mines
Ottawa, Ontario, Canada

NGO conferences

12-14 February 1997
First Session of the Ban Treaty Meeting
Vienna, Austria

25-28 February 1997
Fourth International Campaign to Ban Landmines (ICBL) Conference
Maputo, Mozambique

8-9 March 1997
Association for Aid to Refugees—NGO Tokyo Conference on Anti-Personnel Landmines
Tokyo, Japan

1-12 September 1997
Second Session of the Ban Treaty Meeting
Oslo, Norway

FIGURE 71. *UNICEF-sponsored project teaching boys landmine recognition in Kabul, Afghanistan, 1996.* [UNICEF/HQ 96/0203/Jeremy Hartley]

Chapter 12

Internally displaced people

The forced displacement of civilians has become one of the major humanitarian problems of our time, affecting tens of millions of people around the world. Well over half of this population are internally displaced persons (IDPs), defined as: "persons who have been forced to flee their homes suddenly or unexpectedly in large numbers, as a result of armed conflicts, internal strife, systematic violation of human rights or natural or man-made disasters; and who are within the territory of their own country".[1]

Since the mid-1980s, the number of IDPs in the world has increased dramatically, rising at least five-fold between 1984-1994. Although the quality and availability of data vary, the number of IDPs appears to have peaked in 1994 at above 25 million, declining somewhat since then. Depending on definitions and sources, IDPs are currently estimated as at least 19.7 million, and possibly as high as 25 million. This is in addition to the 14-16 million global refugees. A large number of IDPs are women, often widows or single mothers; children, many of whom are unaccompanied by their families; and elderly people.[2]

The largest numbers of IDPs are found in Africa, with substantial populations in Europe and South Asia as well. In 1996, more than 10 per cent of the total populations of Angola, Bosnia and Herzegovina, Cyprus, Lebanon, Liberia, Sierra Leone and the Sudan were internally displaced. (See map XII, pages 100 and 101.)

While the needs of IDPs are much like those of other poor and isolated social groups, they have special vulnerabilities as a result of being dislocated from their homes: low mobility, weak social networks and limited wage-earning opportunities. For these reasons, in those countries where the proportion of internally displaced is high, IDPs place an unusually heavy burden on social and economic systems.

The causes and categories of internal displacement

Over the past decade, it is the rising number of internal conflicts—compounded by natural disasters and/or weak state structures—that have been the primary cause of increasing internal displacement. Civilians are forced from their home locales and become internally displaced for a number of reasons:

• *Victims of 'ethnic cleansing'.* If a place of origin comes to be identified by the parties to a conflict with a particularly political, ethnic, religious or other communal affiliation, the residents may be targeted for removal. In this situa-tion, they may be obliged to flee to regions controlled by the government, where they will be subject to attacks by opposition forces, or to areas occupied by the opposition, where they will be considered adversaries by their government and denied access to humanitarian assistance. In recent internal conflicts, ethnic cleansing—removing entire communities from their home locations—has become an increasingly common way to deal with land pressures, economic scarcities, religious differences or perceived historical injustices. The former Yugoslavia, the Caucasus, the Great Lakes region of Central Africa and the Rift Valley in Kenya are recent examples.

• *Victims caught up in armed conflict.* If their places of origin become strategically important in an internal conflict, non-combatant civilians may simply become caught in the cross-fire and seek safety, often illusory, in a less turbulent part of the country. When, in the course of their flight, such involuntary migrants cross a national frontier, they can become refugees. By not crossing into another state, however, their vulnerability can be seriously exacerbated simply by their prior geographic association with the conflict area. When internal conflicts are accompanied by political breakdown and governing authority ceases to exist, the displaced populations are marginalized even further.

• *Victims of natural disasters and the environmentally displaced.* Natural disasters and environmental deterioration arising from pressures on resources can cause substantial population displacements if they deny residents their livelihoods and means of subsistence. The line between natural and human-induced destruction is often difficult to draw, particularly in the case of long-term environmental degradation, since human actions can greatly exacerbate the effects of such natural disasters as drought, floods and desertification. Damaged areas must be restored before the residents can return, and when home areas are completely destroyed, alternative receiving areas need to be made ready to meet the long-term needs of the displaced.

The special problems of IDPs

Whatever the cause, the status of IDPs may, in some instances, be only a phase in the process of expatriation. In the first stage before leaving their country, IDPs may be potential refugees unable to cross the border. They may also be reluctant to expatriate due to political, social or personal reasons, and may seek sanctuary inside their country of origin before choosing to flee into exile. Alternatively, repatriating refugees

---

[1] The Secretary-General's Analytical Report on Internally Displaced Persons (Document E/CN.4/1992/23 of 14 February 1992).
[2] US Committee for Refugees, *World Refugee Survey* (Washington, D.C., annual issues for 1984-1997).

may become internally displaced while attempting to return to their home areas, especially in the case of unorganized return or when places of origin have been occupied by other groups of uprooted populations. Mixed population movements along interstate borders further blur these various groups.

Compared with refugees, however, IDPs have significantly less access to international protection. Since IDPs have not crossed international boundaries, they are not legally entitled to the internationally recognized civil and social rights ensured by the refugee status as defined by the 1951 Convention Relating to the Status of Refugees and the 1967 Protocol thereto. Since IDPs live under the sovereign authority of their Governments, which have the legal responsibility to provide them with protection, they are particularly vulnerable to pressures from these Governments, whether at the national or local level.

Under this circumstance, international intervention is limited, in principle, to supportive actions undertaken with the consent of the country in question. However, in instances where Governments are unable or unwilling to provide protection to their displaced populations, humanitarian organizations have sought to assist IDPs: grounding their right to provide assistance on existing provisions of international humanitarian law to war victims and on human rights treaties. In these cases, humanitarian assistance is given to IDPs despite their Governments, rather than with their Governments' support.

While the scope for the international community to provide protection to the displaced is often restricted, the protection of IDPs is a critical issue. It is not unusual for governments to deny, or at least downplay, their internal displacement problems. At the same time, the displaced are typically highly vulnerable social groups with limited ability to articulate their needs for assistance and protection. Both factors complicate the international community's ability to help them.

Over the past few years, however, IDPs have become more visible on the humanitarian scene, for several reasons. First, as internal conflicts and consequent population displacements became more widely recognized in the early 1990s, the humanitarian community has moved the problem of IDPs to the top of its agenda. Second, internal displacement has become more visible to the general public: some of the recent humanitarian crises that have captured the mass media's attention pinpointed mass migrations, such as in the Great Lakes region of Central Africa and in former Yugoslavia. Third, the magnitude of the phenomenon implies that internal displacement cannot be seen anymore as a minor side-effect of a refugee problem, although situations of internal and external displacement are often mixed.

Institutional developments

There is no single humanitarian agency with a comprehensive global mandate to assist and protect IDPs. There is also no institutionalized system to coordinate assistance to IDPs, either at the headquarters level or in the field. Given this situation, in the 1990s, United Nations agencies and other humanitarian partner organizations have aided the growing number of IDPs, both by actively pursuing their traditional mandates and by expanding their capacities to meet these needs.

Among the United Nations agencies:

- **UNDP** responds to the needs of internally displaced persons primarily in the prevention and resettlement phases: earmarking resources for countries beset by disasters or complex emergencies which have substantial displaced populations.

- **UNHCR** becomes involved with IDPs in conflict situations, depending upon a case-by-case extension of its mandate to include the problem of IDPs. It acts by limiting outflows as far as possible and encouraging their return to home communities.

- **UNICEF** assists children wherever they are rendered vulnerable, whether because they are refugees, internally displaced, affected by conflict or natural disasters, inequity or poverty.

- **WFP** assists IDPs with relief food distribution, rehabilitation, recovery and/or development programmes provided through governments or NGOs.

- **WHO**, at the request of governments or the United Nations, furnishes emergency health services and facilities to particular groups, including IDPs.

Among non-United Nations organizations:

- **ICRC** plays a key role, since IDPs are at the core of its mandate to protect all victims of armed conflict. In carrying out its mandate to such victims, including IDPs, the ICRC provides the following kinds of assistance: protection of the civilian population; visits to detainees; health and medical services, including the supply of potable water; food aid; the provision of shelter and clothing; and the restoration of family ties, including tracing missing persons and arranging for family reunification.

- **IOM**'s mandate, which explicitly mentions assistance to internally displaced persons, is to ensure the orderly migration of persons in need of migration assistance. Through an internal task force established in 1994, IOM has gathered information from its missions around the world on assistance to IDPs, and is currently reviewing a set of policy and operational guidelines to derive basic principles for all IOM activities relating to IDPs.

- Numerous **international NGOs** also assist IDPs in all sectors of humanitarian assistance: food, health, water and sanitation, shelter, etc.

Although rich and variegated, the overall response of the humanitarian community to IDPs has been fragmented and ad hoc. In recognition of this major challenge, several steps have been taken towards a more systemic approach.

In resolution 92/73 (1992), the Commission on Human Rights asked the United Nations Secretary-General to appoint a representative to look into the legal and institutional requirements for more effective assistance and protection to IDPs. Ambassador Francis Deng was appointed to this post in 1992 and serves as the United Nations' primary advocate for IDPs. His assign-

MAP XII

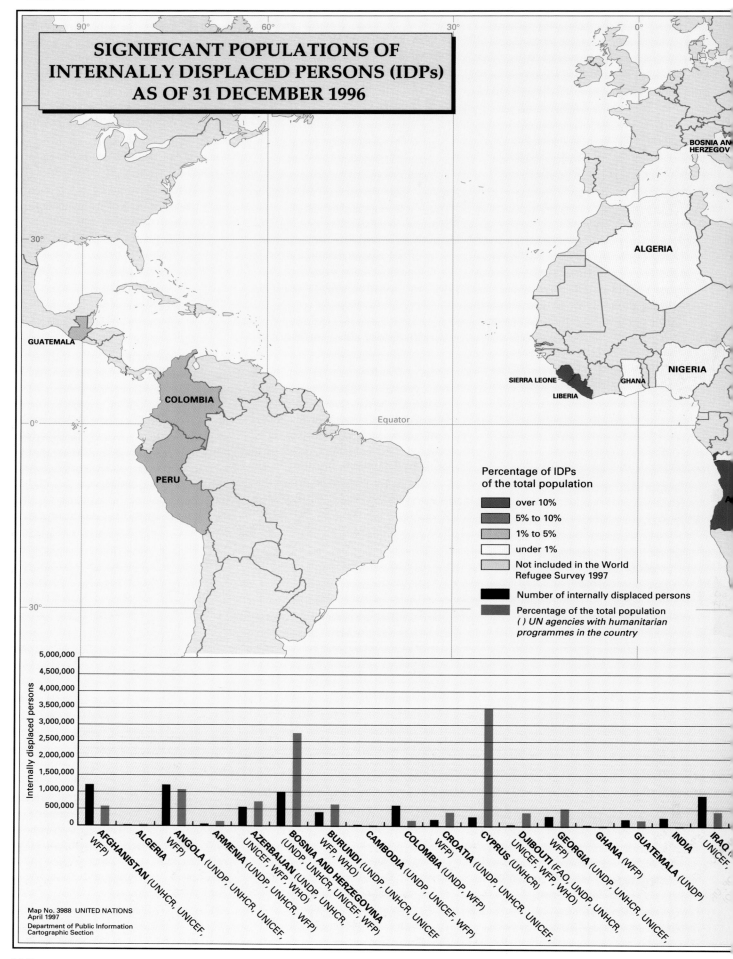

SIGNIFICANT POPULATIONS OF INTERNALLY DISPLACED PERSONS (IDPs) AS OF 31 DECEMBER 1996

ALGERIA

BOSNIA AND HERZEGOV

GUATEMALA

COLOMBIA

PERU

Equator

SIERRA LEONE

LIBERIA

GHANA

NIGERIA

Percentage of IDPs of the total population

- over 10%
- 5% to 10%
- 1% to 5%
- under 1%
- Not included in the World Refugee Survey 1997
- Number of internally displaced persons
- Percentage of the total population
  ( ) UN agencies with humanitarian programmes in the country

Internally displaced persons

5,000,000
4,500,000
4,000,000
3,500,000
3,000,000
2,500,000
2,000,000
1,500,000
1,000,000
500,000
0

AFGHANISTAN (UNHCR, UNICEF,
ALGERIA (
ANGOLA (UNDP, UNHCR, UNICEF,
WFP)
ARMENIA (UNDP, UNHCR, UNICEF,
AZERBAIJAN (UNDP, UNHCR,
UNICEF, WFP, WHO)
BOSNIA AND HERZEGOVINA
(UNDP, UNHCR, UNICEF, WFP)
BURUNDI (UNDP, UNHCR,
WFP, WHO)
CAMBODIA (UNDP, UNHCR, UNICEF
COLOMBIA (UNDP, UNICEF, WFP)
CROATIA (UNDP, UNHCR, WFP)
CYPRUS (UNDP, UNHCR, UNICEF,
DJIBOUTI (FAO, UNDP, UNHCR,
UNICEF, WFP, WHO)
GEORGIA (UNDP, UNHCR,
WFP)
GHANA (WFP)
GUATEMALA (UNDP, UNHCR,
INDIA (UNDP, UNHCR, UNICEF,
IRAQ (
UNICEF,

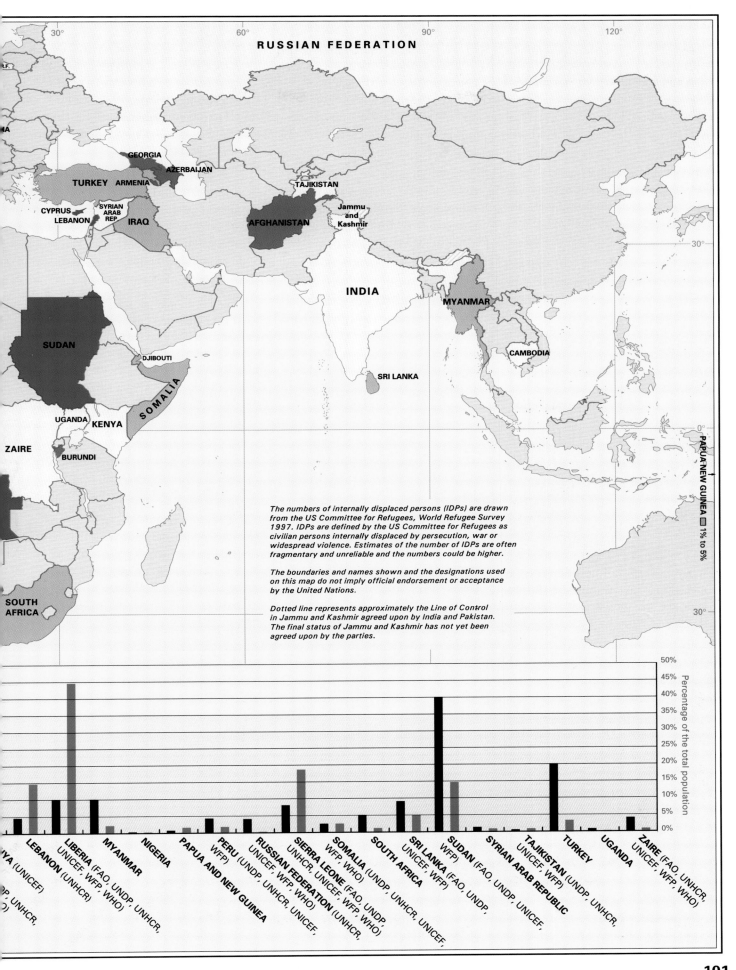

RUSSIAN FEDERATION

The numbers of internally displaced persons (IDPs) are drawn from the US Committee for Refugees, World Refugee Survey 1997. IDPs are defined by the US Committee for Refugees as civilian persons internally displaced by persecution, war or widespread violence. Estimates of the number of IDPs are often fragmentary and unreliable and the numbers could be higher.

The boundaries and names shown and the designations used on this map do not imply official endorsement or acceptance by the United Nations.

Dotted line represents approximately the Line of Control in Jammu and Kashmir agreed upon by India and Pakistan. The final status of Jammu and Kashmir has not yet been agreed upon by the parties.

1% to 5%

Percentage of the total population

ment is to raise awareness about their plight; highlight unmet needs; suggest ways to improve responses in particular countries; develop an appropriate normative framework; and strengthen institutional arrangements.

In December 1994, the Inter-Agency Standing Committee requested the ERC to serve as the United Nations reference point for internal displacement. Shortly thereafter, in July 1995, the Economic and Social Council called upon the United Nations humanitarian system to review its capacity to respond to humanitarian crises and disasters including, *inter alia*, a detailed review of a number of issues relating to IDPs. The IASC, in reviewing this matter through a Task Force on IDPs, has recommended that additional work is needed to ensure a comprehensive and coordinated approach to IDP problems.[3] While deciding that no uniform model can be applied and that the precise structures for assisting IDPs should be determined on a case-by-case basis, the IASC has attempted to clarify the focal points at the headquarters and field levels, as well as operational arrangements, for assisting IDPs.

Measures being considered to strengthen humanitarian response to IDPs include the following:

• The ERC, as Chairman of the IASC, remains the focal point at United Nations Headquarters for the inter-agency coordination of humanitarian assistance to IDPs. Subject to IASC agreement, he is responsible for:

---

[3] The Inter-Agency Task Force on IDPs was established in 1992, with the aim of improving inter-agency collaboration, and subsequently revised its terms of reference in 1995. The Task Force, in addition to the regular IASC membership, has included the Representative of the Secretary-General on IDPs and the High Commissioner for Human Rights. The Task Force has been meeting monthly in Geneva, with secretariat support from DHA.

○ global advocacy on both assistance and protection requirements;

○ resource mobilization and the identification of gaps in resources;

○ management of global information on IDPs; and

○ support to the field on IDP-related humanitarian issues, including negotiation of access to IDP populations.

• The Resident/Humanitarian Coordinator, in consultation with inter-agency country teams, is responsible for coordinating assistance to IDPs, including:

○ addressing IDP's humanitarian requirements before, during and after an emergency;

○ serving as an advocate for the assistance and protection of IDPs;

○ recommending to the ERC a division of operational responsibilities among the agencies; and

○ on a case-by-case basis, also recommending to the ERC that the IASC confirm a lead agency to assume operational responsibilities for IDPs, including camp management where appropriate.

• With regard to operational coordination, there is a continuing need to clarify how agencies divide or mesh their responsibilities for IDPs. In such crucial areas as food aid, rehabilitation programmes, transport and logistics, protection, and human rights, coordination is often addressed through bilateral memoranda of understanding signed by two or more agencies. For example:

○ UNHCR, UNICEF and WHO agreed in a recent Memorandum of Understanding (MOU) that UNICEF and WHO will, respectively, assist displaced women and children and provide health care to IDPs. UNHCR will also be involved,

when requested by a competent organ of the United Nations.

○ UNHCR and WFP agreed in a MOU revised in 1997 to divide their responsibilities for food assistance to IDPs.

In carrying out their operational responsibilities, agencies must take care to distinguish among the needs of differing groups of displaced people. Some IDPs are mixed among resident communities; others gather in camps; still others simply disperse throughout a territory. Interventions in these various settings will tend to have different costs and impacts.

In countries emerging from protracted conflict, one special category of IDPs of great concern to the humanitarian community is demobilized soldiers. (See chapter 8 on demobilization in Angola and Liberia, page 60.) Their displacement is not only from their homes, but also from the basic fabric of society, since they are all too often socially and psychologically alienated from their traditional communities, livelihoods and skills. A large proportion of demobilized soldiers never return to their traditional homelands and, unless they receive targeted reintegration and rehabilitation assistance, they can threaten public security even after the conflict has ended.

While a number of steps have been taken along these lines to strengthen the international institutions aimed at assisting IDPs, much still needs to be done. The challenge which now faces the humanitarian community is not only to ensure that IDPs' basic needs of survival are met, but also to broaden the efforts to prevent human rights abuses, improve governance and promote equitable development practices. Both adequate early warning systems and reintegration measures—addressed to all vulnerable groups in the community—are needed in order to improve the conditions of life for IDPs ∎

Chapter 13

The link between relief and development

FIGURE 72. *Housing reconstruction is a central part of ensuring reintegration of returning refugees in Kibungo Province, Rwanda, April 1997.* [Harald Brandsberg]

General Assembly resolution 46/182 gives an explicit directive that emergency assistance must be provided in ways that will support recovery and long-term development. The resolution clearly recognized the need to establish a strong link between relief and development activities within the assistance community and, in particular, within the United Nations system. It charges the ERC to help orient the interventions of the humanitarian relief community towards longer-term development objectives.

The link between relief and development was initially viewed as a continuum, or linear progression, where relief operations in response to a humanitarian crisis would be followed first by a programme of rehabilitation and then by the resumption of development activities. The concept of a continuum grew out of experiences in providing assistance following sudden-onset, natural disasters. With the upsurge in complex man-made emergencies, however, it became clear that this linear model did not reflect the full scope of relief and development linkages. The implication of the continuum was that

one must wait for the emergency to run its course before initiating rehabilitation and reconstruction work. Yet, in a long-lasting complex emergency, following such a sequence might miss opportunities for initiating and/or accelerating the processes of recovery in the midst of, or emerging from, an internal conflict or other man-made disaster. As an example, at the same time that one must provide essential drugs, medicines and health care to victims of emergencies, there is also a need to train health workers and maintain effective health monitoring systems, if the society is to have any hope of sustaining its own health and medical services.

Relief organizations are increasingly looking at the longer-term consequences of the aid they provide in response to specific crises. Until the dispersal of the camps during the civil conflict in Zaire in late 1996, donor Governments, United Nations agencies and other relief providers expressed strong concern over the long-term impact of maintaining large refugee camps along Rwanda's borders in Zaire, Tanzania and Bu-

rundi. The humanitarian community faced the dilemma of choosing between providing the resources required to maintain the camp populations and providing additional assistance for reconstruction and reintegration inside Rwanda, designed to meet the longer-term needs of the Rwandan population.

Aligning development objectives with humanitarian principles

In the post-cold-war environment, development has come to emphasize the active promotion of civil society, democracy, liberal economic policies, and structures that protect human rights. There is a growing consensus that international assistance should bridge the twin objectives of emergency relief and economic and civic development. For example, by ensuring that life-saving food aid does not undermine local agricultural markets, donors can maximize the longer-term development as well as the humanitarian impacts of their assistance.

While the primary focus of humanitarian relief agencies is to save lives, they also have the responsibility to foster national or local capacities to cope with long-term needs. As the flow of relief ebbs, it is essential to ensure that the community, through local or national mechanisms, has the means to secure its survival and to provide for its long-term stability. Relief, provided without considering how to build local capacity, often fosters long-term dependency. In addition, where the structures of a society have broken down, there is a danger that humanitarian assistance can serve to strengthen or restore fundamentally flawed structures in the society, thereby perpetuating, or even accentuating, the social, economic and/or political inequalities which triggered the conflict in the first place. Relief organizations have struggled to design food and other assistance programmes, like wet feeding or targeted distributions, which reach the most vulnerable groups—most often women, children, the elderly and the disabled—rather than providing more generalized distributions which powerful elements in a population can more easily access. A major challenge in designing humanitarian programmes is to avoid reverting to development and other practices which may have contributed to the original conflict.

The evolving consensus

In July 1995, the Economic and Social Council urged the United Nations humanitarian system to review its capacity to respond to humanitarian crises and disasters and to build relief and development linkages. In response to this request, the IASC has developed an integrated approach to relief and development. This has resulted in:

- a commitment to deliver humanitarian assistance in ways that will ensure recovery is built on the efforts and actions of the people and communities concerned; and
- a common understanding that the processes of recovery should begin during an emergency and that responses to immediate needs created by an emergency must also begin laying the foundations for recovery.

The Administrative Committee on Coordination (ACC)—chaired by the United Nations Secretary-General and composed of executive heads of programmes and specialized agencies of the United Nations system—has emphasized that relief and development programmes must overcome whatever divisions have been created by the earlier separation of their approaches, budgets and functions. The ACC has endorsed the need for an integrated and coordinated framework to address any combination of political, military, humanitarian, human rights, environmental, economic, social, cultural and demographic factors in situations of crisis. The ACC has also emphasized that this integrated approach linking relief and development should be adopted during both crisis and post-crisis conditions, and involve partnerships with non-United Nations actors, particularly, local and national authorities.

The evolving consensus in the United Nations system has resulted in a commitment to focus on strengthening local capacities and coping mechanisms in post-conflict United Nations relief operations. This model of intervention states that, rather than relying primarily on international organizations, first priority should be given to strengthening and working through local institutions.

Despite this evolving consensus within the relief and development communities, there remain very practical challenges to linking relief and development operations in conflict situations. Institutional structures within and outside the United Nations system have specific relief and development responsibilities. New working relationships and understandings need to be developed across the United Nations system to ensure that primacy is given to strengthening local capacities.

The IASC has begun focusing on this critical issue of capacity building in the context of linking relief and development. By its nature, successful local capacity building will involve a rethinking of the relationship between the humanitarian providers and the recipient populations. For the external actors responding to an emergency, a central task must be to identify, understand and seek to strengthen whatever coping mechanisms victims draw on during their time of crisis. This will require identification of local coping mechanisms and evaluation of their viability and value for the society. Relief programmes must then seek to address immediate needs while helping to strengthen these mechanisms and, thereby, laying the foundation for recovery.

The move from ''pure relief'' to ''relief tied to recovery'' can only take hold in a climate of improving security, where processes of reconciliation are already underway. At the same time, however, it is critical that the political and security negotiations embrace, even at the earliest stage, the need for economic and social recovery. WFP food-for-work projects often provide food in exchange for labour to jump-start the rebuilding of essential infrastructure —water, sanitation, schools, etc.— that is a prerequisite for development. Small capacity-building projects undertaken by UNICEF targeting women's groups in Afghanistan have been successful in limiting the long-term dependency of this generally vulnerable group. (See box on gender issues in Afghanistan, page 48.) Demobilization and reintegration programmes in Liberia and Angola are intended to help both combatants and civilians to reestablish basic livelihoods and hence contribute to longer-term stability. In countries impacted by landmines, such as Afghanistan, Angola, Bosnia and Herzegovina or Cambodia, early demining of agricultural lands is essential if local inhabitants are to return to self-sufficiency.

Considerable responsibility is placed on the United Nations Humanitarian/Resident Coordinator to ensure that these relationships are fostered. In recognition of this responsibility, DHA and UNDP convened a workshop during April 1997 in Turin, Italy, to enhance the collective understanding of the roles and responsibilities of the Humanitarian/Resident Coordinator in fusing relief and development objectives. The

FIGURE 73. *Reconstruction of a sewer under way in Sierra Leone, August 1996.*

FIGURE 74. *A health worker speaking about basic health and nutrition as women and children await vaccinations in Balkh, Afghanistan, June 1996.* [UNICEF/HQ 96-0212/Jeremy Hartley]

workshop stressed the importance of elaborating a broad strategic framework at the outset of a crisis which would address both immediate humanitarian and longer-term development goals. Subsequently, the IASC has decided to deploy joint teams to Afghanistan and Mozambique to test this approach.

A further challenge is financing. Donor Governments have traditionally separated relief from development in their assistance programmes. Furthermore, donors often provide humanitarian relief unconditionally, whereas development assistance is becoming increasingly tied to specific objectives or is otherwise conditioned. The overall decline in international aid resources from donor countries has led to increased competition for resources among the assistance community. It also appears that projects which bridge relief and development do not readily attract donor support. (See box overleaf.)

DHA—together with all the humanitarian agencies—has followed these trends closely and is discussing with the donor community how to better support both relief and devel-

opment activities. For such an approach to work, DHA believes that funds for critical development activities should be provided with the same flexibility, in terms of allocation and disbursement, as funds for relief activities. This follows the recommendation made in the Joint

Evaluation of Emergency Assistance to Rwanda which states that the international donor community should, "develop rapid and flexible procedures for disbursing reconstruction funds along the same lines as procedures for emergency assistance." For example, funding and other support for the strengthening or reestablishment of the security apparatus and the law enforcement system constitute critical components of recovery. When linked to demobilization of combatants, these are pivotal activities which must be undertaken at the earliest opportunity, once conflict begins to abate.

As the United Nations develops greater understanding of the issues surrounding the resolution of complex emergencies, approaches which seek to bridge relief and development are being explored. It is essential that, in this process, the interests and concerns of those affected are not overlooked. Ultimately, no amount of change and adaptation by the international assistance system can replace the willingness of communities themselves to determine how best to improve their own situation and prospects ∎

FIGURE 75. *IDPs building a community oven after conflict ended in Mozambique, Serra Choa Manica Province.* [UNICEF/DOI 94-1270/Giacomo Pirozzi]

South Caucasus (Armenia, Azerbaijan and Georgia): resource constraints on relief and development

DHA began its activities in the South Caucasus in late 1992, as a result of the conflicts in the Nagorno-Karabakh region of Azerbaijan, and in the Abkhazia and South Ossetia regions of Georgia. Spillover from the conflicts caused humanitarian emergencies in both countries, as well as in Armenia, and created more than 1.5 million refugees and internally displaced persons. International humanitarian assistance was particularly important as these countries were confronted with the collapse of their economies following their independence from the Soviet Union.

Although peace settlements still seem distant, cease-fires are holding. The three countries have gained a fair level of stability, and are showing signs of renewal and growth. In sum, the overall situation for the majority of the population in the three countries has improved considerably from the 1992-1993 crisis period, although not yet to the levels reached during the former Soviet era.

At the regional meeting held in March 1996 in Tbilisi, Georgia, United Nations agencies, donors and NGOs decided that the United Nations CAP for the region should include not only emergency relief programmes, but also transition programmes bridging relief and development. As a result, US$ 61 million out of US$ 111 million for the 1996-1997 Appeal for the Caucasus, launched on 30 May 1996, was earmarked for transition programmes. As of the mid-term review meeting in November 1996, the overall donor response was 40 per cent, and the transition programmes had only attracted 31 per cent of the requirements. As of the end of March 1997, only 50 per cent of the total Appeal requirements had been received. It remains difficult to attract support for the humanitarian situation in the Caucasus—the health and education sectors have received almost no funds—and very challenging to raise funds for the transition programmes.

DHA representatives in the field

as of 17 March 1997

Afghanistan—Mr. Alfredo Witschi-Cestari
United Nations Humanitarian Coordinator, UNOCHA,
and United Nations Resident Coordinator
Islamabad
Tel.:   92-51-253789
Fax: 92-51-261460

Angola—Mr. Ramiro Lopes da Silva
United Nations Humanitarian Coordinator and
Director, UCAH
Angola
Tel.:   244-2-348-205
    244-2-341-072
Fax: 244-2-342-710

Armenia—Mr. Robert Robinson
UNHCR Representative and DHA Coordinator
Yerevan
Tel.:   3742-151749
E-mail: undha@arminco.com
Fax: 3742-151749

Azerbaijan—Mr. Paolo Lembo
DHA Coordinator and
United Nations Resident Coordinator
Baku
Tel.:   99412-921857
E-mail: root@dhafcu.baku.az
Fax: 99412-983235

Burundi—Mr. Mirza Hussain Khan
United Nations Humanitarian Coordinator and
United Nations Resident Coordinator
Bujumbura
Tel.:   257-223135
Fax: 257-225850

Cote d'Ivoire—Mr. Jamie Wickens
Regional Focal Point for Coordination
Abidjan
Tel.:   225-211709
    225-216335
Fax: 225-226349

East Africa—Ms. Patricia Banks
Coordinator
Integrated Regional Information Network (IRIN)
Nairobi
Tel.:   254-2-622147
Fax: 254-2-622129

Ethiopia—Mr. Alieu Sallah
UNDP Resident Representative and United Nations
Resident Coordinator
Addis Ababa
Tel.:   251-1-511025/7
Fax: 251-1-514599
    251-1-515147

Georgia—Mr. Marco Borsotti
United Nations Humanitarian Coordinator and
United Nations Resident Coordinator
Tbilisi
Tel.:   99532-943163
E-mail: toby@undha.org.ge
Fax: 99532-959516

Great Lakes—Mr. Pierce Gerety
United Nations Humanitarian Coordinator for the
Great Lakes Region
Nairobi
Tel.:   254-2-622672
Fax: 254-2-622632

Iraq—Mr. Staffan de Mistura
UN Humanitarian Coordinator in Iraq
Baghdad
Tel.:   964-1-774-5721
    964-1-774-5703/4/5/6/7

Liberia—Mr. Tesema Negash
United Nations Humanitarian Coordinator
Monrovia
Tel.:   231-226-041/2
Fax: 231-226210

North Korea (DPRK)—Mr. Christian Lemaire
United Nations Resident Coordinator
Pyongyang
Tel.:   850-2381-7566
Fax: 850-2381-7603

Russian Federation—Mr. Christopher Carpenter
DHA Coordinator and
United Nations Resident Coordinator
Moscow
Tel.:   7095-284-3220
Fax: 7095-973-1960

Rwanda—Mr. Omar Bakhet
United Nations Humanitarian Coordinator and
United Nations Resident Coordinator
Kigali
Tel.:   250-75381
    250-76906
    250-72796
    250-73360
Fax: 250-73360

Sierra Leone—Ms. Elizabeth Lwanga
United Nations Humanitarian Coordinator and
United Nations Resident Coordinator
Freetown
Tel.:   232-22-225311
Fax: 232-22-223250

Somalia—Mr. Dominik Langenbacher
United Nations Humanitarian Coordinator and
United Nations Resident Coordinator
(*based in Nairobi*)
Tel.:   254-2-226408
Fax: 254-2-217483

Sudan—Mr. Christoph Jaeger
United Nations Coordinator for Emergency and
Relief Operations (UNCERO) and
United Nations Resident Coordinator
Khartoum
Tel.:   249-11-780565
Fax: 249-11-773128
    871-151-6741
    873-161-0441

Tajikistan—Mr. Markku Visapaa
United Nations Resident Coordinator
Dushanbe
Tel.:   7-3772-210679
Fax: 7-3772-510084

Zaire—Mr. Aliou Diallo
United Nations Resident Coordinator
Kinshasa
Tel.:   243-1233424/5
    243-1233431
Fax: 243-8843675
    243-1233431
    871-150-3261

Recent DHA publications and training materials

I. *DHA News*: a quarterly publication on humanitarian issues

No. 22	Women in Emergencies	April/May 1997
No. 21	Tools for Disaster Response	December 1996/January 1997
No. 20	WorldAid'96	September/October 1996
No. 19	Humanitarian Assistance and the Transition Issue	June/August 1996
No. 18	Disasters and Development	April/May 1996

II. Manuals

Disaster Management Training Programme (DMTP)
Recent training modules and trainer's guides:
—Introduction to Hazards (3rd edition) (1997)
—Emergency Information Management and Telecommunications (1997)
—Guidelines for Trainers Leading Disaster Management Workshops (1997)
—The Disaster Management Training Programme (1997)
—International Law of Disasters and Armed Conflict (1996, 1997)
—Logistics (1997)
—Disaster Management Ethics (1996)

Experience and Lessons Learned from the Management of Major Disasters (sales publication)
—Mudflows (Volume I) 1997

III. Monographs

Emergency Stockpiles Information for Workers in the Humanitarian Field:
—Model Agreement on Customs Facilitations (1996)
—Model Agreement between United Nations and Governments (1996)

Search and Rescue Activities - Information:
—Natural/Sudden Onset Disasters Involvement in 1996: Statistical Summary (1997)
—United Nations Disaster Assessment and Coordination Team (UNDAC) Report—
South Pacific Training Course, 1996 (1997)
—International Search and Rescue Advisory Group (INSARAG)—
Report on Meeting of Leaders of International Search and Rescue Teams (September 1996)

IV. United Nations Consolidated Inter-Agency Appeals for Complex Emergencies

Published in 1997
—Albania
—Angola
—Bosnia and Herzegovina
—Chechnya, Russian Federation
—Democratic People's Republic of Korea (DPRK)
—Great Lakes Region
—Sierra Leone
—Somalia
—Sudan

Published in 1996
—Afghanistan
—Angola
—Bosnia and Herzegovina, Croatia, Federal Republic of Yugoslavia, Former Yugoslav Republic of Macedonia and Slovenia
—Caucasus (Armenia, Azerbaijan and Georgia)
—Chechnya, Russian Federation
—Democratic People's Republic of Korea (DPRK)
—Great Lakes Region
—Iraq

—Lebanon
—Liberia
—Sierra Leone
—Somalia
—Sudan
—Tajikistan

V. International Decade for Natural Disaster Reduction (IDNDR) publications

—Stop Disasters (quarterly)
—Economic Aspects of Natural Disasters (1996)
—Cities at Risk (1996)
—Legal Aspects of Natural Disaster Prevention (1996)
—The IDNDR Video Catalogue (1996)

Documents and technical reports are printed in limited numbers and will be provided on request subject to their availability by DHA Geneva.

To request, contact: Publications Unit, Room C.215
Palais des Nations
1211 Geneva 10
Switzerland.

Direct line: 917 2704
Facsimile: (+41 22) 917 0023
E-mail: dhagva@dha.unicc.org

Printed in France
GE.97-01682–July 1997–9,000

DHA/97/72

United Nations publication
Sales No. GV.E.97.0.11

ISBN 92-1-100745-3